A MESSAGE TO MY SUPPORTERS

Dear friend and partner,

The best thing about this book is that it is true. This is not a work of fiction. It is the record of mighty acts of the Holy Spirit as He has moved upon hungry hearts, especially in the former Soviet Union.

While the talented and generous writer has named the book, *John Carter: The Authorised Biography,* this is really in my opinion a misnomer. A more appropriate title would have been, "The Acts of the Holy Spirit." I was just fortunate enough, in the providence of God, to be in the right place at the right time. The Holy Spirit is the hero here.

Furthermore, a subtitle could have been added: "The Amazing Miracles That Happened When Thousands of Christians Worked Together." While that title may have been a bit long, it certainly would have told the truth. You see, dear friend, none of these miracles would have happened without you and others like you. Your prayers and gifts brought salvation to thousands. I, therefore, dedicate these heartwarming stories to you. This is your book.

I also record here the grateful thanks of my heart. I thank God for the privilege of preaching His Word. I thank you for your partnership in the gospel.

May God wonderfully bless you..

John Carter
President
The Carter Report, Inc
Arcadia, California

"I was stunned when I saw tens of thousands of Russians night after night storm the giant Palace of Sport to hear the Spirit-filled preaching of Pastor Carter. I saw thousands of Communists and atheists give their lives to Christ. I saw thousands baptised in a single day. This was one of the greatest experiences of my life. Read the book and marvel at God's power."—*Danny Shelton, president, Three Angels Broadcasting Network*

"It was a cold winter morning of 1992. John Carter arrived by train and on the first day of our acquaintance announced his dream—we shall baptise 2000 people in Nizhni Novgorod. We could hardly believe that, but this dynamic preacher set our hearts on fire. I believe this book about God's miracles in Russia and Ukraine will burn the flame in your hearts—to finish God's work on earth and meet our dream, the second coming of our Lord. It will tell you about a person who became my dearest friend, John Carter, the preacher, the pastor, and modern apostle of Christ whose only desire in his life is to save the lost."—*Vasily Stolyar, president, West Russian Union Conference, Moscow, Russia*

"Sometimes people in the church ask me, who influenced your spiritual life the most? Undoubtedly I answer, Elder John Carter. Happy is the minister who had a good instructor, mentor and tutor and helped him mature. I matured as a person and a minister by the side of this great Adventist evangelist. I believe the book about his life will help readers, especially the young people to grasp a vision of their lives in the latter days of the world. I pray that this edition will reap a harvest of new John Carters to finish the preaching of the gospel."—*Vadim Butov, Russian evangelist*

"Anyone who reads this fascinating book and is not moved should check if they still have a pulse. John and Beverley Carter's ministry has touched thousands of lives, and made Seventh-day Adventist Christians of my wife and myself. But this book is no mere history: it is a challenge to Christian readers that they, too, should do their individual part in fulfilling Jesus' command to go into 'all the world' and share the good news."—*Mark Kellner, journalist, Silver Spring, Maryland, USA*

"For years I have been urging John Carter to record his experiences as an Adventist evangelist. For many years he has run programs in different countries with incredible results. The experiences he has had working with people at every level of society and the dramatic ways God has got him through difficult times are stories that should not be lost. This book will give inspiration and vision to others to attempt and expect great things from God."—*Dr Graeme Bradford, research fellow, Avondale College, Australia*

JOHN CARTER

JOHN CARTER

THE AUTHORISED
BIOGRAPHY BY
PHIL WARD

SIGNS
PUBLISHING
COMPANY

Printed and published by
Signs Publishing Company
Victoria, Australia

Bible quotations in the book have been translated by the author.

Photographs in this book are courtesy of John Carter, Graeme Bradford, Bob Pease, Susan Piraino and Bob Ludwig, and are used with permission.

Additional copies of this book are available by visiting www.adventistbookcenter.com

This book was
Edited by Graeme H Brown and Nathan Brown
Designed by Jason Piez
Cover pictures by The Carter Report, Inc
Cover design by Shane Winfield
Typeset in 12/18 ITC Legacy Serif

ISBN 1 876010 98 3

About the author

Phil Ward is a journalist with a passion for reaching secular people with the gospel. In the 1970s, Phil wrote the scripts for John Carter's first television series in Albury, Australia. In the 1980s he wrote groundbreaking 30-second religious TV commercials. These attracted record crowds to evangelistic programs in Sydney, Melbourne, Brisbane, Canberra, Launceston and Perth. Versions of these ads aired on television in Africa, the United States, New Zealand, Russia and Ukraine. They set evangelistic attendance records in each of those areas.

Phil has spent a lifetime writing. He was the producer of a five-night-a-week television program and has been the editor of several newspapers.

At present, he is focused on producing a new translation of the Bible. When not struggling with the meaning of Hebrew and Greek words, he also spends time as the writer of the newsletter "Evangelism News."

Contents

1800 PEOPLE BAPTISED IN ONE DAY

A bitterly cold Friday night in Russia. John Carter is more uncertain than he has ever been in his life. He's a Seventh-day Adventist minister, and tomorrow he will baptise 1800 people. This has never happened to him before. In fact, it has probably never happened to any Adventist minister before. And he doesn't know if baptising 1800 people is the right thing to do.

Just four weeks earlier, these people had been atheists and Communists. Now they want to be Christians. And Carter isn't sure their conversions are genuine. He's experienced at running evangelistic campaigns in Western countries. Most of these series have run for six or nine months. And most of them have produced 50, 100, 300 or so baptisms. But here in Russia, 1800 people want to be baptised after hearing him preach for only four weeks.

There's a knot in Carter's stomach, so he decides to take a walk. He tells his wife he needs fresh air. And he walks out of the run-down Russian hotel into air that is not just fresh, but freezing.

There's a lot of traffic flowing on the Russian roads. And there are still hundreds of pedestrians. He walks along looking at everything and nothing, hearing everything and nothing. Then among the depressed and miserable faces he sees a face that seems to shine. The man walking on the other side of the road is clearly different from the others. He looks so happy, Carter can't help but notice him. Then the man sees Carter. In broken English, he calls out, "Pastor Carter! Pastor Carter!"

The man wears a fur-skin hat pulled down over his ears, and a thick, drab, Russian coat to keep out the bitter cold. In his hand he holds a Bible wrapped in newspaper. His face beams with delight. He makes his way across the road as fast as the traffic allows. He waves his hands as he talks. Steam pours from his mouth as he speaks.

"Pastor Carter! Pastor Carter!" They are the only words he can say in English. But he mimes his message. "Tomorrow is the happiest day of my life! Tomorrow I am being baptised."

Carter knows this is not a chance meeting. This is a message from God, saying, "Yes, John, it's all right to baptise those 1800 people tomorrow."

An hour earlier, Carter and his wife, Beverley, had been driven back to their hotel after the evening meeting finished. At the same time, the man with the Bible wrapped in newspaper also left the stadium. He faced a long walk home through a city where, even at midnight, the cars don't turn on their headlights. At the sports stadium, he had been one of 6500 people watching and listening to the evangelist. From where he sat, Carter was just a small speck on the stage.

Now, after walking for an hour, he sees John Carter only a few lanes of traffic away. This is his chance to speak to him personally. He rushes across the road through a procession of vehicles seemingly determined to stop him. He meets the preacher face to face and mimes out his joy: "Tomorrow is the happiest day of my life!"

The two men give each other a great Russian bear hug. And now Carter's face is shining too. His aimless walk has ended. He strides back to the dingy hotel room with new purpose. This "chance" encounter has not only changed his mood; it has changed his life forever. He cannot speak a word of Russian, but he is about to become the most successful evangelist the Russian people have ever had.

The next morning, a convoy of buses leaves the city's sports stadium and slowly weaves its way toward the Volga, Russia's most famous river. Police give the fleet of 30 buses safe passage across the city. The Russian Army is already at the river, pitching tents for use as dressing rooms. (They did their work for free. The only payment, a Russian Bible to each soldier.) The army parks one of their large trucks in a central position to use as a stage for the preacher. The soldiers stack ammunition boxes on top of each other to make a set of stairs to their "stage." It takes a lot of organisation to baptise 1800 people.

The police haven't been asked to escort the convoy. They've taken it on themselves. This is astonishing because the police protecting today's convoy are the same police officers who had "visited" the local Adventist church two years earlier. About 50 church members had been present. The police bashed and beat some members in front of the others. And they smashed the furniture. There was no particular reason, except the police were anti-Christian.

But how different their attitude today! The police car is driving along in front of the convoy with loudspeakers blaring. Travelling in the car behind, Carter asks his translator what the police loudspeakers are saying. They wind their car window down so the translator can hear it. The translator says, "Stop the traffic. Stop the traffic. Make way for these Christian Adventists who are coming to baptise their people. Make way. Make way."

It is June 6, 1992. What is happening today could not have happened 10—or even two—years earlier. During the 70 years of Communist rule, Christian baptisms were small, quiet and usually secret occasions. But Mother Russia has decided to give her people freedom. Now the police, the army and the government bus company are all helping 1800 Russian people obey Jesus' command to be baptised.

There is no official count of how many spectators are here today—possibly 5000, maybe even as many as 20,000. They range from the curious to the committed. For several days the Russian media have reported what was going to happen. So crowds of people are gathering on the grassy banks of the Volga to see another extraordinary day in the turbulent history of Russia.

The baptism could easily become a debacle. But the crowds stay quiet, intent on what they are watching. Despite the massive size of the spectacle, it remains a calm, quiet and reverent Christian baptism.

The long winter is over. It's the end of spring. There are no longer large slabs of ice flowing down the Volga River. But, even for the Russians, it's a cool day. Carter is used to the balmy weather of California and Australia, so he will find the water extraordinarily cold. He delivers his sermon from the back of the truck, and then about 30 pastors walk into the fast-flowing river. They stand almost waist-deep, about five metres (five yards) apart in a straight line facing the shore. Then 30 new Russian Christians step into the water. Each baptismal candidate walks out to a pastor, who says a few private words in Russian.

From the truck, Carter calls out, "In the name of the Father, the Son, and the Holy Spirit." His translator repeats the words in Russian, and then each of the 30 pastors lowers a newborn Christian completely under the water. Another 30 walk out to repeat the process, then another 30. It continues for an hour.

This is all new to the Russian people. They have never seen a public baptism, so they don't know how to dress. Several young women are baptised wearing their wedding dresses. Russian war veterans walk into the water wearing their medals. Some veterans have been victims of landmines in the war in Afghanistan. They are carried into the river to be baptised.

Toward the end of the ceremony, John Carter himself walks into the water to baptise a few people who speak English. He says words of encouragement to them, and then lowers them into the Volga.

The next day the newspaper runs a double-page story about the event. It uses the headline "The Return of John the Baptist."

This is not the only baptism that will take place during Carter's six-week preaching program here in the city of Gorky (now called Nizhni Novgorod). Another baptism will be held the next Sabbath, and another a week later at the end of the final program. On these three occasions, a total of 2530 people will dedicate themselves to God through baptism. It is the largest baptism by any religious denomination in Russia's history.

If there were a larger venue in the city of Gorky, there may have been even more people baptised. The Palace of Sport has seating for only 6500 people. By running the same program four times on the opening weekend, and having 1000 people standing in each session, the opening program caters for about 30,000. But at least 20,000 people cannot get into the opening program.

5

An American TV crew from 3ABN is astonished by the crowds being turned away. They go outside the stadium to video it. Their most poignant footage is of an old Russian man dressed almost in rags. He calls out, "Let me in. I've been waiting 70 years for Jesus. Please don't make me wait any longer."

The crowds are a problem for the city authorities. They are afraid the people outside the hall might riot because they cannot get in. But Carter's team tells them there will probably be a bigger public outcry if they close down the meetings. So the authorities let the meetings continue, calling in the Russian military's crack security personnel to control the crowds. And some of these soldiers start listening to the meetings and are also baptised.

A few weeks earlier the city authorities had told Carter his program wouldn't attract an audience. "The Russian people are not interested in religion," they said. Those same city authorities now realise they had misjudged the situation; the people want religion more than any of them imagined. The city officials who said it wouldn't work, now tell him, "God sent you here."

On the third night of the meetings, Carter asks the audience, "How many here suffer from depression? How many of you feel that life is filled with blackness and despair? Do you wonder if life has any purpose or any meaning? Could you please raise your hand?" At least 95 per cent of those in the audience raise their hands. Looking at their faces you can see it is true: Communism has left them very unhappy.

Carter offers his audience what they regarded as an incredible treasure. They can have a free Bible if they attend seven meetings. The Carter team will give away 25,000 Bibles while in Gorky.

But many people don't want to wait to read the Scriptures.

The team loans Bibles to people to use during the meetings and thousands of people start arriving several hours early so they can read the Bibles before the meeting starts.

The Bible might be almost 2000 years old, but to the Russian people in 1992, it is new and exciting. The people regard it so highly that when they receive their Bibles, they protect them by carrying them wrapped in newspaper. These Bibles are thick because Russia doesn't yet have the thin paper used to print Bibles in the West. Each night thousands of people walk into the stadium carrying these large, precious bundles in newsprint.

For Elder Carter, one of the most unforgettable moments is inviting 6500 Russians to open their Bibles to John 3:16. He has them read the verse in unison in their native language: "For God so loved the world that he gave his only begotten Son, so that whoever believes in him will not perish, but will have eternal life." In the West, these words move us, but we are somewhat used to them. In Russia, they've never heard the words before. There are tears everywhere across the vast stadium floor.

It is amazing to watch the changing body language of the people attending these meetings. The first night the people sit incredibly still. There is no fidgeting, no movement. Hardly one face in 1000 is smiling. Four weeks later, it is astonishing to walk into the TV editing room to compare this audience with video of the opening night. Now almost everyone is smiling. Some are laughing. Some even have large bunches of flowers they carry forward and place on the stage. The video of the crowd four weeks later shows constant small movements of thousands of people. It's as if Christianity has given them the freedom to fidget, permission to be themselves.

Some nights you cannot see the stage because of the covering of flowers. Beverley Carter takes one or two bunches home, and the next day she takes the rest to children's hospitals and orphanages to brighten up the rooms.

The pressure of six weeks of preaching is hard on John. To give him occasional days off, fellow Australian evangelist Graeme Bradford takes three or four of the evening programs. One night when Bradford takes the meeting, he suggests to Carter they get the audience to sing. "Up to this time they haven't been singing. But Russians are full of music. I think these people are ready to sing," he says.

They teach the audience the Russian version of the song, "People need the Lord." "It really matches their experience because times are so hard and tough for them," says Bradford. The singing is not particularly good the first time they try it. However, the Carter team persists and the singing gets better and better. As their confidence in Christ grows, their confidence in singing increases.

Under the Communists, this city was called "Gorky." Ironically, the Russian word *gorky* means "bitter." And that's what life was like for its inhabitants during the Communist period. But for thousands of people, the bitterness is now ending at these meetings.

During the Communist era, Gorky was home to a training college for the Department of Internal Security—the internal version of the infamous KGB. Members of the city's Adventist church were often victims of Internal Security. Now the shackles have been removed, they should no longer be worried—but old habits die hard.

The church members are deeply suspicious when the general in charge of the Internal Security College wants Carter to pay him a visit. Carter arrives at the college with several of his senior team members and his son, David, as a cameraman. They are ushered into a spacious dining room where they eat with the general and several colonels. The general says he wants Carter to tell the students of the college about Christianity.

At the end of the meal, the General and his staff toast Carter with vodka. He says to Carter, "You need some good vodka so you can be strong and preach to my men."

"I have a power much stronger than vodka," Carter replies. "I'll introduce you to it soon."

Carter and his entourage are led into a large auditorium, filled with 1000 solemn but expectant and attentive young atheists wearing uniforms reminiscent of Hitler's SS. A generation earlier the young people who sat in this room went out across Russia to persecute Christians. Now he has 60 minutes to win this generation to Christianity. It is the first time a Christian minister has ever preached to the KGB.

When introducing Carter, the general says he has been attending the meetings at the Palace of Sport. Now he wants his students to hear some of the things he has heard.

Carter tells these 1000 young men and women they are children of God. Speaking though his translator, he argues that the Russian people can have true freedom only when they realise they are God's children. He is thinking on his feet. He wants to make the most of the opportunity and wants the momentum to continue after he has gone.

He has a Bible and his team members have a few more Bibles. While standing there talking, he develops an idea of how to switch the allegiance of these young Communists to the Bible. He ends his meeting by presenting a Bible to the general as his personal gift. Then he announces that he will provide a Bible for all the college staff members and for each of the 1000 students.

There are tears in many eyes in the audience. Some are so impressed that they start attending the sports stadium meetings. And in a few weeks time, some of these Internal Security trainees will be baptised as Christians.

CHRISTIANITY COMES TO RUSSIAN TV

John Carter's Gorky evangelism series didn't just introduce spirituality to thousands of atheists. It also changed Russian television. Carter gave Russia its first regular Christian TV program—and he also introduced the concept of commercials to local TV.

During the Communist era, there were no advertisements on TV. John Carter was the first person to purchase advertising time on Gorky's local station. Because they had never sold advertising before, the Gorky TV station didn't know how much to charge. They even asked Carter himself how much he should pay for the advertising campaign.

When the TV executives found out how many spots *The Carter Report* wanted, they raised a serious question: "We don't have that many spaces between programs in one night. How can we show that many advertisements?"

"Stop the programs halfway through, and show the commercial

in the pauses," Carter suggested. And that is how John Carter introduced the concept of a "commercial break" to Russian television.

Having advertising on TV wasn't just a new concept for station executives; it was also a new experience for viewers. One viewer rang the station to say, "I have already seen that announcement several times. Why are you showing it again?"

The idea that an advertisement needed to be shown repeatedly for maximum impact was not an idea that had crossed the mind of that viewer.

The impact of the advertising in this city of two million people was dramatic. It produced the largest audience to attend any public meeting in the city's 800-year history.

And how much did the Carter team pay for this remarkably effective advertising campaign? They simply gave the TV station cameras for its newsroom.

The local station couldn't afford to buy cameras to video events for its evening news service. So Carter gave the station two amateur video cameras to pay for the advertising. Both Carter and the TV station thought it was a good deal.

For several nights, while preaching in the Gorky stadium, Carter saw a Russian TV crew filming with professional equipment. After three days, they asked him for an interview. He found out they were not from the local station, but from Moscow TV, 400 kilometres (250 miles) away. News stories about Carter's meetings on the local Gorky media were being repeated nationwide. So Moscow TV came to film a documentary for the nationwide network.

The young interviewer told Carter his program was making a national impact. "I have attended many political rallies. But the crowds here seeking God are the biggest crowds I have ever seen," the interviewer said. The 30-minute documentary they produced was very favourable to Christianity—and was shown in prime time in every city in Russia.

"We were almost overwhelmed when we sat down to watch it," Elder Carter said later. "It was biased, very biased, in favour of the gospel and the work we were doing. It looked like a 30-minute promo for Christian evangelism. We were amazed that journalists, just out of Communism, produced a program that so strongly supported the good news. It made you feel like crying and praying and praising God all at the same time."

The climax of the documentary was the baptism. It showed church pastors baptising thousands of people in the Volga River. When still-wet new Christians with happy smiles came out of the water, the TV crew interviewed them. These new Christians enthusiastically testified on national TV about God's power to save. About 50 million people saw that program.

This was the second time John Carter featured on nationwide Russian TV. The previous year he gave a 15-minute explanation of Christianity on *Good Evening Moscow*. This was broadcast on every Russian-language TV station in the then-USSR.

Carter has been making progress on Russian TV. In just 12 months he has broken new ground on TV four times. The next step is a Carter TV program, and this marks two other firsts for Russia. It is the first time someone buys an entire timeslot to run their own program. And it's the first time a program produced by a Christian church was shown on Russian TV.

Video of Carter's meetings were broadcast on Saturday afternoons with the title *The Living Word*. One person who saw the program was the First Secretary of the Communist Party, an extremely important person in the Russian system. Vladimir Samorodkin was in charge of 630 government-owned factories. The factories he supervised made nuclear submarines, Volga cars and trucks, rockets that could detect and destroy America's stealth bombers, tanks and world-famous Mig fighter jets. Comrade Vladimir had a beautiful wife, a luxury apartment, a chauffeured limousine, a large salary and all the perks of high office. But he didn't have Christ.

It was a coincidence the first time Vladimir and his wife, Valentina, watched *The Living Word.* They didn't sit down to view a religious TV program. But when it came on, they found it fascinating. Carter was explaining Bible prophecies proving Jesus is the Messiah.

Vladimir had never seen anything like this in his life. He was so impressed that he made sure his Saturday afternoons remained free so he could see subsequent programs. The couple watched for several months. The Holy Spirit gradually convicted them.

At the end of one program they called the phone number on the screen and were invited to attend a Christian Adventist Church meeting. (In Russia, Seventh-day Adventists are called "Christian Adventists.") A few months later he and his wife were baptised. Today, Vladimir is a powerful preacher and a church elder.

✳ ✳ ✳

Danny Shelton, the founder of 3ABN television, is part of the Carter team here in 1992. He is destined to become perhaps the best known Adventist church member in the world and 3ABN will become one of the largest Christian TV networks in North America. But that's in the future.

At Carter's meetings in Gorky, Shelton catches a new vision. Carter has opened the door by getting religious programs onto

Russian TV. Shelton wants to keep the momentum rolling. He wants to produce more Christian programs for Russian TV. But where can he do it?

Before the Carter meetings in Gorky, the local Christian Adventist church had only 120 members. Now they are about to baptise 2530 more. In one of the team meetings, a local church leader points out the obvious: "There is not enough room where the local church meets for all the new members." The team decides they must buy or build a church. Danny Shelton takes it on himself to raise the money.

The city of Gorky is built on two levels: one on a hill, the other on the flat. In the lower area they find a block of land with a partly built centre for Communist youth. Like many buildings in Russia, it has sat there for years uncompleted. It looks more like a building destroyed by bombs than a youth centre.

At first, the asking price is about $US300,000. Negotiations continue and they buy it for $US100,000. Viewers of 3ABN then donate more than $US1 million dollars to construct a building on the site. The construction project was originally expected to take 12 months. However, nothing works that well in Russia. Construction took 40 months but when it was complete, they had a local conference administration office, a church with seating for 1000 people and—much to Shelton's satisfaction—a TV production centre. The complex is the largest Protestant building in Russia.

Fifteen years later, most of those who work at this TV centre are people baptised in that 1992 campaign in Gorky. The centre produces world-class programs that have won international awards. The people who make the programs are young, creative and spiritual. There are not many religious shows in any language better than theirs. The programs they produce are broadcast on 170 TV stations across Russia, Ukraine, Georgia, Moldova and other Russian-speaking countries.

FIREBOMB THE MEETINGS

O ne of the main characters in the Bible was a man called Saul of Tarsus. When the Christian church was in its infancy, he worked with the religious leaders to persecute Christians. But while making an international trip to organise further persecution, he was converted (see Acts 9:1-19).

A priest in Gorky is about to have a similar experience. Just like Saul, he is strongly opposed to the new religion in his city. He feels he has to make a stand against it. Like Saul, he wants to stop it, or at least to disrupt it.

His first step is to try to disrupt the Carter team's advertising. Carter has paid for advertising billboards and signs on and in every bus and railway carriage. The priest organises teams to destroy these signs. Often the posters are pulled down only five minutes after being put up.

This priest also organises other priests to stand outside the opening meeting, trying to convince people not to attend. But they stop only a few people from entering. Thousands still attend the meeting.

However, this priest has planned a "punishment" for those who ignore the blockade. Anyone who goes inside will face the danger of a smoke-and-fire bomb. The priest can't allow himself to be seen behind such an illegal act. So he arranges for a few young people to throw the bomb for him.

The Palace of Sport that day is absolutely full. Some 8000 people are in the auditorium. There is no way for people to escape because 1500 people are standing in the aisles. If the people in the audience panic and run for the doors, hundreds could be trampled to death. But that doesn't seem to matter to the priest and his cronies.

John Carter and his translator are speaking when the bomb is thrown onto the stage. It belches out thick, choking smoke, then bursts into flame. Carter keeps preaching, realising he needs to distract the audience so they won't panic.

The thick smoke engulfs the stage and starts to choke Carter and the translator. The curtains begin to catch alight. The conference president and Carter's driver rush onto the stage and throw water on the flames and onto the bomb. Carter keeps preaching. The smoke slowly clears. The crisis is over.

This is the first full-scale evangelistic program Carter has led in the former USSR. If the firebomb had scared him off from preaching in Russia, the future of the church would have been dramatically different.

But the persecution doesn't stop. The groups of priests continue to gather at the doors, intimidating those who enter.

After a few weeks, Carter forms a strong friendship with the governor of the province. He tells the governor what is happening. The governor calls the police, and the police send these troublemakers on their way.

For several years Carter returns to this city once or twice a year to hold public meetings. On every trip this priest develops another unpleasant "welcome" for him. He is a man on a mission of hate.

Eventually the priest decides to prepare an exposé of these misguided Protestants. He gathers all the Carter videos and audio cassettes he can find and collects Christian Adventist books. Then he starts to go through them, searching for the evil they contain.

Day by day, long into the night, he plays the tapes and reads the books. But the more he studies them, the more he realises they are right. Heaven's light begins to shine into his mind.

Eventually, he picks up a telephone and calls the Christian Adventist Church office. The repentant priest asks if Carter can baptise him. Today he is a faithful and proud member of the church he used to persecute.

THE FIRST MARTYR

A young man from Gorky was the first martyr among the Russians John Carter won to Christ. His father was a KGB officer and he himself was a member of the Mafia. He was in the first group of people baptised at a Carter campaign in the former USSR.

After being baptised, the young man went to tell his Mafia colleagues what had happened to him. He wanted them also to discover the joy he had found in Christ. However, they disapproved of him being baptised. His punishment was death.

There have probably been more Adventist martyrs in the USSR than in any other country. And martyrdom did not end when the Soviet era ended. But as Tertullian wrote in the days of the early church, "The blood of the martyrs is the seed of the church."

The young man's mother had also been baptised. She preached for six hours at his funeral, opening up the story of redemption to the mourners. Even KGB friends of her husband had never heard a political speech to match this speech! When she finished speaking, she asked people to stand up to show they wanted to turn to God. Fifty people stood—all because of his death.

On her son's tombstone, she wrote the Russian words of John 3:16:

"For God so loved the world that he gave his only begotten Son, so that whoever believes in him will not perish, but will have eternal life."

In a cemetery full of memorials expressing hopelessness, this tombstone is one of hope. The mother also had engraved on the tombstone the words, "Until I see you again, my son."

When John Carter first came to preach in Gorky, the city had only just opened up to visitors from the West. It had been a closed city during the era of Communism, where military products were developed and manufactured. Foreigners were officially banned from the city to protect the secrets of military research.

Carter's meetings in Gorky made a remarkable long-term change to this city. So many people became Christian Adventists that today the government classifies it as Russia's only major city with a large Christian Adventist presence. Today, Russia's fourth largest city is probably the "Protestant capital" of Russia. It certainly is the "Adventist capital."

When it was established in 1221, the city was named Nizhni (pronounced *Niz-nee*) Novgorod. It owes its prominence today to its former insignificance. When the Tartars invaded Russia 700 years ago, they destroyed all the major cities. But new, insignificant towns like Moscow and Nizhni Novgorod were spared. These then grew to become major centres.

By 1850 Nizhni was the most important city for trade in Russia. By 1900 it was one of the country's most important industrial cities. The world's first convention centre was built in Nizhni Novgorod.

The Communists renamed the city Gorky in 1932, but it reverted to its former name when Communism fell in 1991.

Visiting the city today, you can meet many people who attended Carter's meetings.

Sergei was a drug addict and a member of the Russian Mafia. He and two other Mafia members attended Carter's meetings. God touched the hearts of these hardened, professional criminals. When Carter made an appeal for people to accept Christ and renounce sin, all three walked forward. The Mafia leaders were not happy about this. They threatened all three with death unless they renounced their faith.

The other two men buckled and went back to their life of crime, which eventually led to their deaths. But Sergei remained true to his decision. Despite the threats, he was baptised, forgiven by Heaven. Then an amazing thing happened: he was also forgiven by his former Mafia bosses. They allowed him to live. Today Sergei is an elder in the church, and runs his own business.

Dr Julia Outkina is another of those who discovered Christianity in the first Gorky series. Her brother was the governor of the province and later became the deputy speaker of the Russian parliament. Julia holds a doctor of philosophy in linguistics. She came to hear John Carter speak because of her professional interest in English.

About five weeks after the six-week series started, Carter and his team were invited to meet with the governor. The governor told him the meetings had had the impact of a magnitude seven earthquake. At the end of the meeting Elder Carter met Julia, the governor's sister. Her finger was bandaged. She told him she had been attending the meetings, but had refused to keep the Sabbath. Instead, she deliberately went shopping on Sabbath.

Later in the day she injured her finger preparing the food she had purchased. She later said, "Every time I held up my finger, it said to me, 'Remember the Sabbath day to keep it holy.'" So, the next

Sabbath she was baptised, making her incredibly happy.

The following year she became Carter's translator when he returned to Gorky for another evangelistic series. Today, she is in charge of the Russian TV production centre operated by 3ABN in Nizhni. She is known nationally as the host of a Christian TV program called *Face to Face*.

Helen was a slender 15-year-old girl when she was baptised in 1992. She later went to university and trained as a doctor. She married a young Christian Adventist minister, Vadim Butov, who now works as John Carter's translator. Their love for people made them volunteer for one of the toughest pastoral jobs in Russia—they went to Siberia.

On the coldest nights they organised their church members to patrol the snow to find drunks and old people who had fallen over. They took them back to the church to thaw out their bodies. If they didn't find them quickly enough, frostbite may take over and they may need their arms or legs amputated. In the morning, Helen, Vadim and the church members would share the gospel, wanting to save the souls of people whose arms and legs they had saved.

In Siberia, Helen earned about $US7.50 a week. And of that, she gave $1.50 to the church she loves. Helen has also become a preacher—one of only two Adventist women holding evangelistic campaigns in Russia. She says she is called by God to preach. She regularly goes into small towns and runs campaigns based on Carter's program. And her campaigns usually produce 50-60 baptisms.

Rashid was probably the least promising candidate to present himself for baptism in Gorky. He was so drunk when he came to the first meeting, he could barely walk. He staggered into the meeting, reeking of vodka, which was unpleasant for the person sitting next to him. Somehow John Carter's message penetrated his drunken stupor and he came back the next night. But he was drunk again. In fact, there wasn't a single night of the program when he didn't stagger in drunk. Despite his state, he walked forward when Carter called for people who wanted to give their lives to God. And when Carter preached about baptism, he committed himself to be baptised.

On the night before his baptism, Rashid vowed he would never drink again. But when he woke up in the morning and started walking around the house, the temptation was overwhelming. He took a bottle out of the refrigerator and started drinking. Even though the baptism was in the morning, he was already thoroughly drunk before it began. The pastors at the bank of the Volga River refused to baptise him.

However, he protested strongly. "I came to *all* the meetings! I *must* be baptised," he pleaded.

The pastors relented and he staggered into the water for baptism. After he was baptised, he kept getting drunk for about a week. Then he gathered his resolve and with God's power gave up both smoking and drinking. Despite his unpromising start, he has stayed in the church. Now he is a faithful church member.

Stanislav Kivochuch is an engineer who makes top-secret navigation equipment for spacecraft. He knows so many state secrets that even 15 years after the fall of Communism, he is not allowed to hold a passport. He will never be allowed to leave Russia.

He was an atheist. He came to the third night of Carter's meetings attracted by the archaeology advertising. He was staggered by what he heard and astonished by what Carter said about God's love. He went home, knelt in prayer and burst out crying. It was the first time he had cried in his adult life.

His prayer was as poignant as it is humorous. "God," he said through his tears, "I don't know if You exist, but it's so great that You love us."

After that, he came to every meeting. He was in the first group to be baptised. In the years since, he has read an average of 10 chapters of the Bible each day, meaning he has read the entire Bible 38 times. But reading the Bible has now become a race against time. He is an albino, with white hair and blue eyes, and like most albinos, he is slowly going blind. Doctors expect the day will soon come when he can no longer read. But he is praying God will let him keep his vision so he can keep reading his Bible.

His religion has not just been academic. He's had the joy of seeing many of his contacts baptised. At a recent evangelistic campaign in his area, he personally knocked on 3000 doors inviting people to attend. Statistically, for every 1500 people invited, one will be baptised. So for his Herculean effort of knocking on all those doors, another two people probably joined the church.

Dimitri Bulatov was a guitar player in a punk rock band when he came to Carter's 1992 meetings. A whole bunch of punks came, and Dimitri and a few other punks were baptised. He dedicated his life to God, then trained as a minister. Now he is a conference youth leader. He still plays in a band but now it's a band of Adventist young people providing music for youth programs. Dimitri was one of 25 people baptised in that first evangelistic series who later became ordained Adventist ministers.

Alexander Sinitsin was the lightweight boxing champion of Gorky. He had performed in the city's Palace of Sport many times. But when he came to the Palace of Sport to hear Carter, it was his turn to be knocked out. He was so astonished he came to the meetings every night. He was baptised and he also became a minister.

As a pastor, he is an incredible innovator. He studies everything he can find to get new ideas on how to make the church grow. He often holds seminars for other Russian pastors, helping them to grow in their faith. Today, Alexander is the pastor of the Volga Auto Plant church, a church built by finance from *The Carter Report.*

Igor, Victor and *Uri* were three Russian soldiers. Igor came to the third-last meeting in Gorky. He was so impressed he brought two friends the next night. On the final night, Carter summarised every meeting he had taken for the entire series. The three soldiers were impressed with what they heard. When an appeal was made to be baptised, they made the commitment.

Carter and his team had no idea the trio had attended so few meetings. Had he known, Carter later said, he wouldn't have baptised them. But God knew better. All three have remained true to their commitment and remained close friends. Working together they have nurtured a new congregation just outside the city of Dzerzinsk

Once, while still in the army, Victor was with four other soldiers on a field trip. Their truck became hopelessly bogged in deep snow. An office went to get an army tank to pull the truck out. Victor was praying that God would free the truck. The other soldiers started mocking him. "Make us laugh," they said. "Show us what a Christian can do!" So he did. Victor—and God—shocked them all when Victor got behind the wheel and drove the truck out of the bog as if there was no snow at all.

On one occasion, John Carter was with all three of these former soldiers on an overnight train trip. The three gathered a group in the corridor outside his sleeping compartment. As he was falling asleep, he heard the trio teaching the group about Christ's second coming. When he woke six hours later, they were talking about the blessings of paying tithe.

Vadim was already a church member when Carter ran his first Gorky program. But a miracle happened to him at the meetings. Vadim stood out among the thousands of people in the meetings because he was a hunchback. He was so stooped, he was almost bent double. He found it difficult to breathe and talk. His arms moved out of sync with the rest of his body. Carter couldn't help notice him.

However, as he came to the meetings each night, his body slowly changed. When Carter first perceived this gradual change, he thought it was his imagination. But night after night, Vadim's body grew a little straighter. By the end of the six-week program, he was no longer a hunchback. He was now so healthy he was enthusiastically carrying camera equipment for the Carter cameramen.

Vadim has stayed faithful to the God who healed both his soul and body. He grew in grace and became the custodian of his local church.

Olga was a young girl in a Ukraine village when the Germans invaded in World War II. When the Germans retreated, her village was accused of assisting the Germans. So the Communists decided to kill all 1000 villagers. A bulldozer dug a huge pit, large enough to hold everyone from the village. All the people were ordered to strip naked and walk into this giant grave. Machine guns then started spitting their venom to kill everyone. Olga and a young boy decided to try to escape and ran naked into the nearby forest. After several days of freezing cold, she acquired some clothes. Then she caught a train north to Gorky.

A few years later she married. But during Stalin's purges there was a knock on her door. They took away her husband and she never saw him or heard of him again. For the next 40 years she was a complete unbeliever with no family, no joy and no hope. Something attracted her to the Carter meetings and in her darkness and despair she saw light.

"I have waited 50 years for this day," she said. "I now have hope, I now have love, and I now have joy."

Today, she has not lost that joy. She is one of the oldest members in her local congregation—and one of the happiest.

Yuri Maslov is a very tall man, but served on a Russian nuclear submarine, usually a task for short men. When he retired from the sea, he began working in a factory building nuclear submarines in Gorky. He also became a gross drunkard. He beat his wife and child so badly they left him.

Still a drunkard, Yuri attended Carter's second series of meetings in Gorky. He went only for fun, but he was impressed by what he heard. Three baptisms were scheduled to be held at those meetings. They were at the end of the fourth, fifth and sixth weeks of the program. Yuri played a part in all three of those baptisms.

He was baptised at the first baptism, and afterwards he went to tell his drunkard father. They celebrated his baptism by both getting drunk together. Then for the next week Yuri took his father to the meetings, and at the end of that week his father was baptised. They again celebrated with a liberal dose of vodka.

During the final week, Yuri took his mother and sister to the meetings. Then on the last day of the meetings, they also were baptised. This was followed by the obligatory alcoholic celebration— a habit Yuri and his family have fortunately dropped.

A year later Yuri invited a woman on the street to attend Carter's third series of meetings in the city. She came and accepted the Lord. She soon became his new wife.

About two years after Yuri was converted, he became the manager of the Adventist Book Centre in the city. He has made it the most prosperous Adventist Book Centre in Russia. Ten years later, Russian-born evangelist Vadim Butov held an evangelistic series in the city. Yuri visited his former wife and daughter and invited them to the meetings. They were astonished at what a fine man he had become.

"I would never have believed that Yuri would become a person like this," his former wife said. Because of the dramatic change in Yuri's life, his daughter and former wife decided to attend the meetings. After the program they joined a baptismal class, studying Bible subjects to prepare them for baptism. They were both baptised.

Unfortunately, not every story about someone baptised in this city has a happy ending. Some people have walked away from their commitment.

Ludmilla was the mother of the young man martyred by the Mafia. She preached the six-hour sermon at his funeral. God used Ludmilla that day. For several years she continued spreading the gospel. She was always doing good deeds, especially caring for victims of cancer.

But a group of legalists came to Gorky with a "false gospel." They told her that Christians had to be as perfect as their Saviour. Ludmilla was caught up in this heretical teaching and left her first love.

The fire in her heart went out, much to the delight of her KGB husband. Years later it was still a bitter loss to Carter. "I will never cease to pray that when Christ returns, Ludmilla will be there to throw her arms around her son," he says.

Stanislav Lapshin was a criminal, a pickpocket and a heroin addict. He was a member of the Mafia gang who killed Ludmilla's son. He was, however, out of town on the day of the murder.

One day he went to his friend's grave and read the words of John 3:16 on the tombstone. He was so moved by what he read he went to visit Ludmilla. And when Carter returned to the city to take a second series of meetings, he attended them and was baptised.

A year later, he became a pastor. Because the church was growing so rapidly, most trainee pastors went straight to work and did their training by correspondence. In Stanislav's case, this was an excellent idea because his time was to be short.

He threw himself into his work. He was part of a group that organised the first widespread evangelistic magazine in the USSR. It's called *Hidden Treasure*, with a circulation of half a million. Church members buy it for 10 cents a copy and give it to their friends.

Before he was baptised, Stanislav contracted hepatitis C, a disease common among heroin addicts. He worked hard to bring many of his fellow drug addicts into the church. Most of them are now dead, either from AIDS or hepatitis C. But they all died in the Lord.

Natasha, Stanislav's girlfriend, and he stopped living together the day after he had been baptised. However, she also became a church member and the couple married. She now works full-time for the church as the conference president's secretary. When they were first married, the doctors said, "You won't be able to have children." However, they had a son. This 11-year-old is now one of the most involved children in his church. Despite his young age, he teaches the weekly Sabbath school lesson to children younger than himself. He wants to be a pastor like his father.

Stanislav served as a minister for only 12 years. The deadly hepatitis C he contracted as a heroin addict eventually claimed him. The young pastor died at age 33.

OLD DOG, NEW TRICKS

Usually it's young people who come up with harebrained ideas that most people think won't work. It can be totally unexpected when such ideas come from an "old dog." But the late Marvin McCalpin was an "old dog" who came up with a new trick at John Carter's Gorky meetings.

Marvin, an American, was a talented musician. He was impressed by the idea of Carter running an evangelistic series in Russia, even though it was an unproven concept. He made a significant donation toward the meetings in Gorky. But Marvin didn't just give his money. He gave himself. He came to Gorky to work as part of the Carter team.

Being on the team didn't take as much time as Marvin may have expected. With time on his hands, he decided to do a little sightseeing. Sixty kilometres (40 miles) from Gorky, he found a city named after a founder of the KGB. The city stinks from the deadly fumes of dangerous chemicals, used in the production of the USSR's chemical weapons. It remains a centre for modern Russia's chemical industry and is considered the worst polluted city in the former USSR. The life expectancy here is only 45 years. It's hard to see anything attractive about this city. But Marvin came back full of excitement.

"John, you must hold meetings in Dzerzinsk!" he exclaimed to Carter, to whom the name meant nothing.

"It's not practical," Carter insisted. "I can't leave what I'm doing here to go over there."

But Marvin didn't give up and John gave in. "All right! All right! I'll do it," he said. "But I can only do it for one day. For the other nights you'll have to use the videotapes from the Shrine Auditorium."

The Shrine Auditorium is the venue in Los Angeles that hosted the Academy Awards. When Carter moved to California in 1990, he held a series of 17 evangelistic meeting in this famous venue. An amazing 24,000 people attended the opening program. Every program was filmed for TV. Before going to Russia, Carter's team had taken these 17 videos and dubbed them with a Russian translation. These were what Marvin would have to use if he wanted to run his program in Dzerzinsk.

Marvin spent $US1000 on this "harebrained" project. His only advertising was some posters and a few banners saying the meetings would start the next Sunday. He booked a local theatre. And then he prayed that people would come.

When Carter arrived at the theatre on Sunday, he couldn't get inside. To everyone's surprise except Marvin's, there were 2000 people crowded around the door of a theatre that seated only 1700. They held two identical sessions to accommodate the crowds.

Carter took the same program there as the opening meeting at Gorky. When it finished, he explained to the audience that he couldn't be with them in person for the next two weeks. However, they would set up a video projector with a giant screen to show videos of his meetings. To everyone's surprise—except Marvin's—the crowd kept coming back.

When the video series ended, Carter personally returned to Dzerzinsk to take a second "live" meeting. He called for those who wanted to be Christians to come forward. One thousand people walked toward the stage. This was beyond everyone's wildest dreams—except Marvin's.

Unfortunately, the team was not geared to cope with a response of 1000 people. But they coped as best they could. The final result was that the Carter team baptised 130 people in Dzerzinsk and established the only Protestant congregation in the city.

A few months later, Carter's Gorky team manager, Pastor Graeme Bradford, returned to the city. With the help of newly baptised young people, he held a series of three meetings. Fifty people came to the first meeting. Those people told their friends about it, so the next meeting had 100 people. Those 100 then told their friends, and there were 200 at the third meeting.

The local Dzerzinsk church members were excited about their new-found faith. They started constructing a new church building, financed by two Australians, Laurie and Hazel Jones. And while most things in Russia take a long time to happen, this 300-seat church was finished only two years after the evangelists first came to town.

✳ ✳ ✳

One thousand kilometres (600 miles) to the south is a Mafia leader who has a private army of 400 thugs. They are armed to the teeth. He is the most feared man in the region.

No-one knows how it happened, but copies of the videos from Dzerzinsk somehow travel 1000 kilometres south. The Mafia boss watches them and is converted. He is so astonished by what he discovers on the tapes that he orders his thugs to watch them too. Some of them are also converted.

The Mafia man gives up his life of crime. But that is not all he gives up. He has a giant home, a mansion, the largest house in the city, built on the profits of violence and drugs. But he now sees a more urgent need than having a mansion to live in. He sells his house and uses the money to build a church.

Everyone in that city is astounded. In fact, the man is well known for hundreds of kilometres around. People are amazed by his changed life. He spends large amounts of time spreading the gospel.

Two years later, Carter returns to Gorky to dedicate a new church at the Volga car factory. The former Mafia leader learns Carter is there. He drives the 1000 kilometres (600 miles) north to see him. His first words when he sees Carter are, "It's really you!" He has seen him many times. In fact, Carter has led him to his conversion. But until now every time he has seen him, it was only on a screen.

"It's really you," he blurts out. Then he reveals the reason for his journey. "I need your help to get materials and videos so I can preach."

The former Mafia boss has now become a legitimate businessman. But more importantly, he also has become a soul winner for Christ. He now gives people Bible studies. He's engaged in spreading the Word. He loves advancing the cause of the everlasting gospel.

DECLARE A STATE OF EMERGENCY!

O ne million colour brochures roll off a printing press in Texas. The presses run around the clock for several days. Every few minutes, the printers remove random sheets to check the print quality. But they cannot read a word of what they have printed. It is all typed in a foreign language. They are printing brochures that will lead to one of the largest baptisms in the history of the Christian church.

Christianity began in 31 AD when 3000 people were baptised in Jerusalem. The Christian religion has rarely matched the success of its opening day. For many centuries Christians have dreamed of seeing results like that again. And now it's about to happen. John Carter is about to step on board a Delta Airlines jet to fly from Los Angeles to the city of Kiev. And before he steps on a plane to fly back home, almost 3500 people will have been baptised.

This will not be easy. Three years earlier, when he preached in Nizhni, his program baptised 2530 new believers. But the powers of darkness and political figures will fight to try to prevent this happening again.

The Kiev program will be based on the successful program in Gorky three years earlier. Like Gorky, this program will be held in the city's biggest stadium, the Palace of Sport. Like Gorky, the meetings in Kiev will be promoted with high-quality brochures church members will deliver to every home. Like Gorky, TV commercials will show Carter standing at famous sites in ancient Egypt, encouraging people to attend. But this will be on a larger scale than the meetings in Gorky.

It has taken six months to organise these meetings—and almost every step has been a battle. Before the USSR split into 15 separate republics four years earlier, the Soviet Government had a "Ministry of Religion." On the surface, it may have seemed this government department was to promote religion. But it was actually there to control and subdue it. The newly formed independent nation of Ukraine has inherited a "Ministry of Religion"—and the old attitudes continue.

Each time church leaders in Kiev try to arrange the permits necessary to hold the Carter meetings, another obstacle is thrown in their way. The leaders are at their wits' end. What can they do to win over the Minister of Religion? Someone suggests an almost impossible idea: "Let's get a petition signed by each Christian religion operating in Kiev."

Could something like that happen? The leaders of each denomination don't have the time or inclination to help another denomination. But the Christian Adventist leaders have no other option.

They write their petition and take it to the Baptists—and they sign it. They take it to the leaders of the Pentecostal churches—and they sign it. They take it to the Catholic bishop—and he signs it. They take it to a leader of the Russian Orthodox Church—and he signs it. One by one, almost all the denominational leaders sign the petition.

With the signatures of so many religious leaders, the city's mayor and the Minister of Religion now sign the authorisation. The meetings can go ahead. In a few weeks time, both the mayor and the Minister of Religion will change their minds. But it is too late. Their signatures are on the authorisation forms.

The venue will be the Kiev Palace of Sport, a centre of Mafia activity. Twelve months after Carter's program, the Australian national wrestling team will compete in this same venue. The Kiev Mafia leader will come to watch them wrestle, surrounded by a dozen men with submachine guns. The Mafia is so much in control here they don't worry about overseas sporting stars or media seeing their weapons. Since the Mafia is so involved in sport, it is a brave move by Carter to use the Palaces of Sport in the various cities he visits.

A bigger problem than the Mafia in Kiev is the archbishop of the largest church. This man is strongly opposed to Protestants. Several months before the meetings, he decreed the Carter program must be stopped. "It will never happen, except over my dead body," he said. And that is what happened. He was in robust health, but 10 days before the meetings started, he suddenly dropped dead. This left opposition to the Carter programs in disarray and the meetings were able to start with little hostility. However, his spirit of opposition continued in some of those who survived him.

Kiev's Palace of Sport seats 9500 people. By holding three identical opening sessions, 28,500 people can attend. But will they come? During the past four years, all the major Christian churches have held public meetings in Kiev. Has the novelty of Christian public meetings worn off?

Carter is concerned. He has what entertainers call "opening-night jitters." Will the people come? At 8.30 in the morning, he goes to the venue. It is eight hours before the program is due to start but 1000 people are camped at the front door. Carter's concern starts to ease. If that many people are there so early, the program will probably succeed—and it does.

For the first session alone, about 100,000 people come to the Palace of Sport—but there is seating for only 9500 of them. An extra 3000 people pack the hall, standing shoulder to shoulder. Despite the large numbers crammed inside the hall, it hardly seems to have reduced the numbers outside. The pressure of the crowd shatters seven glass doors in the Palace of Sport.

The huge number of people create an exceptional crowd-control problem. The city officials declare a state of emergency, allowing them to take extraordinary measures to reduce the numbers coming to the meetings. They close the closest railway stations so people who want to come to the meetings cannot get off the trains. But people keep pouring into the city centre. The other two opening meetings seat 9500 people, with 3000 standing. And at least 100,000 people are turned away. This is heartbreaking for the Carter team.

But with the huge crowds, the opposition also grows. The local leaders of the Christian Adventist Church are summoned to appear at City Hall. "Your meetings are illegal," the Minister of Religion tells them. "You are teaching religion; that is not permitted. You are creating a public disturbance; that is against our laws. You are teaching children to pray; that is forbidden. You are covering the city with your advertising; that must cease. We are issuing orders. Stop the preaching! Stop the meetings!"

The president of the church in Kiev responds with a calm, yet firm reply. "We have broken no laws," he tells the minister. "We are abiding by the country's constitution. We will not close down the meetings. By God's grace, we will complete our mission."

That evening, both the 5 pm and 7 pm meetings go ahead as scheduled. To the public everything seems normal, but the future of the meetings is under a dark cloud.

The next morning, Carter and some of his volunteer helpers from Canada, Australia and the United States visit the embassies of these three Western nations. They want their diplomats to pressure Ukrainian authorities to allow the meetings to continue. The United States Ambassador takes up their cause, but he doesn't just leave it for subordinates to handle. He personally contacts senior officials in the Ukrainian Government. He tells them the Kiev city authorities are operating outside the laws of Ukraine and the United Nations. The Australian Consul General also lobbies intensely on their behalf.

Despite pleas from the diplomats, and from local civic and religious liberty groups, official harassment grows worse. Having failed to intimidate the local Ukraine church leadership, the authorities take a different approach. They will try to intimidate Carter himself. If they can get rid of him, the meetings will automatically stop. They will try to run the preacher out of town.

Carter is summoned to City Hall to meet the Minister of Religion face to face. No church administrators are allowed to go with him or to advise him. Only his translator, Igor, stands with him.

The local church leadership is worried. Carter, having lived almost all his life in Australia and the United States (which have genuine religious freedom), has never experienced anything like this. Will he buckle under the pressure? Will these former Communists make his life so uncomfortable he will want to leave as soon as possible?

Two other issues worry church leaders. First, Carter doesn't know the local laws. The city officials can make claims about the legality of some small point and he wouldn't know whether they're telling the truth. Second, what if the authorities throw Carter in jail? If they imprison him and his translator for a few days, the meetings would be so disrupted it would be difficult to resume after they are released.

This is serious. The success of the project and to a large degree the future of the Protestant church in Kiev now depends on just one man. Could the city officials bluff John Carter into leaving? The minds of the church leaders alternate between worry and prayer.

Inside the office in City Hall, Carter faces a barrage of demands and accusations. "You are ordered to close down the meetings," the minister says.

"But what about the people who are coming?" Carter asks. "What about the government contract?"

"You are winning too many people to your religion. Close down the meetings," the minister insists.

"We are here with a legally binding contract," Carter responds. "We are here because your government invited us and gave us permission. We have a great responsibility to the thousands who are attending the meetings. You may arrest me if you wish, but we will not close down the meetings."

The Minister of Religion was an old Communist who was not used to being told no. So he repeats his speech. Then Carter repeats his response. The Minister of Religion appears genuinely perplexed. In the past, he has told church officers what to do and they have always done it. Carter is not obeying the rules. This is something he cannot quite understand.

The meeting lasts for about an hour. When logic and persuasion, don't seem to work, the minister makes an implied dark threat: "If you continue these meetings, we cannot guarantee your safety."

Ukrainian church leaders wait for Carter outside the building.

They are more than worried. Has Carter compromised? Has he succumbed to the bullying? They make occasional comments to each other, but most of the time they are praying in silence.

At last, John and Igor emerge. The president of the church for Ukraine meets them there on the footpath and asks what happened.

"I said I would not close down the meetings. They will have to lock me in jail to stop them," Carter reports.

The president is greatly relieved. "Praise the Lord!" he exclaims. "We have all been here praying for you. We thought perhaps you might have compromised the faith."

That night, the two programs continue as if nothing has happened.

However, the government officials are still intent on stopping the meetings. Their next strategy is to exploit a law requiring police attendance at such programs. The Carter team knows this law and has followed it exactly. They have had police present at every meeting. But the city officials hatch a plan.

The police station providing police for the meetings advises the organising committee they can no longer do so. Obviously, their opponents have persuaded the officer in charge of the station.

The Carter team visit another police station: "No, I'm sorry. We can't help you."

They visit another: "No, we can't supply any police for you."

They continue their task of visiting every police station in the city of Kiev. Every answer is no. As rejection follows rejection, they are told every police station has orders not to supply police for the Carter meetings.

As the time for the meeting draws near, the team faces a serious crisis. If they go ahead with the meeting, they have broken the law and given their opponents a legal basis for closing them down. Should they cancel tonight's meeting? That's unthinkable.

The team continues to pray earnestly. They need God to provide an answer almost immediately. Some Ukrainian team members walk the city streets, canvassing every police officer they meet.

One of them finds himself talking to a senior officer, a major, in the Ukrainian Police Force. The church official unburdens his heart to the officer. He tells him everything.

"They shouldn't do that! That's not right. The Ukrainian people need these meetings," the major says. "I will come myself and I will bring my police with me. We will be there tonight and at every meeting until your program ends."

At five o'clock, Carter and his translator walk onto the stage. Police are stationed at various places around the stadium. And the meetings continue if nothing has gone wrong.

Carter's situation in Kiev has become very dangerous. The local church leaders know it. And reports of the danger have even reached the Adventist Church's world headquarters in Washington, DC. The church administrators in the United States are worried Carter is risking death. They send a message for him to return to the safety of the United States. Carter appreciates their concern but doesn't follow their orders. He will not walk away from these people coming each night to drink of the Water of Life.

The next attempt by Carter's opponents to stop the meetings is to use the power and prestige of the city mayor. (In the former USSR, mayors are much more powerful than those in Western countries.) Surprisingly, this is the same mayor who only a few weeks earlier gave official approval for the meetings. He is now enlisted in the fight to prevent the program continuing. And he knows exactly what to do.

The mayor phones the Palace of Sport. "I want the Palace of Sport closed tonight," the mayor tells the stadium manager. "The meetings being held there are illegal. So tonight, do not allow the doors to be opened. They must be kept locked."

A lesser man might have buckled under the pressure of a 90-minute phone call from the mayor. But the stadium manager refuses. He has seen the power and blessing the people are receiving from these meetings each night. "They are not breaking the law," the manager tells the mayor. "You are breaking the law by trying to stop them. They are doing nothing wrong. The doors will be open tonight and they will be open every night."

Again that evening, Carter and his translator walk onto the stage at 5 pm and 7 pm, and the meetings continue as if nothing is wrong.

Almost every day the city officials create another scheme to try to close down the meetings. But the programs continue.

In Ukraine in 1995, churches needed a permit to conduct a baptism. The Minister for Religion has signed a permit to let the baptism go ahead. But the permit says only 100 may be baptised. The Carter team accepts the permit, but says many more than this will be baptised. The church officials can see something really big is about to happen.

Night by night, thousands of former atheists are drawing closer to God. Now is the night for real commitment. Carter asks those who want to be baptised to walk forward to the stage and thousands move toward the platform.

The baptism is scheduled for August 19. Because few people have their own motor cars, the Carter team will need a fleet of buses to carry several thousand baptismal candidates and their friends to the riverside. The city officials are aware of this.

The official at the first bus company the Carter team contacts seems unwilling to help. They phone several other bus companies but it is the same story. On one of their phone calls, they receive a little extra information. "We have been forbidden to supply you with buses. The Kiev Ministry for Religion does not want this baptism to proceed. We will not help you."

On Friday afternoon, with the baptism scheduled for the next day, they still do not have a single bus. The church leaders gather for a prayer meeting. With the deadline upon them, they claim a promise found in the Lord's Prayer: "Give us *this day* our daily bread." They realise this verse doesn't promise to supply their needs weeks or months beforehand. The daily needs are supplied on the day itself.

The next morning, a fleet of 33 large buses pull in at the Kiev Palace of Sport. Each bus runs a shuttle service, making trip after trip between the stadium and the riverbank. On this hot, cloudless day they carry as many as 20,000 people to the river—some to be baptised, some to witness the occasion. But where had the buses come from?

The government officials thought they had stopped every bus. But the Carter team organisers wouldn't rest. They kept phoning further and further afield until they reached further than the government ban had reached. These buses had come from a city some 160 kilometres (100 miles) away.

It's as if the devil knew he had to stop Carter at Kiev—or he would never stop him. But as strong as the satanic powers might be, the power of God is greater. Carter goes on to become the most successful evangelist the Protestant church in Russia and Ukraine has ever seen. Statistics produced in 2005 reveal how effective the Carter team becomes. They show that for the previous five years, the team is responsible for 60 per cent of all Christian Adventist evangelistic baptisms in the former USSR.

Christianity first arrived in what became the USSR in 988 AD. It happened in Kiev where Carter is now preaching. Prince Vladimir decreed that his people must become Christians. Hundreds of people were taken to the Dnieper River to be baptised. Now, 1000 years later, a fleet of buses takes people to the same river in the same city for the same purpose.

Three separate sessions are arranged to baptise people coming to the meetings in Kiev. In the first session, 50 Ukrainian pastors baptise 2817 new Christians. The team decides the second session four days later will not be as public as the first. This will minimise problems with the city authorities by using an indoor swimming pool on a Wednesday night.

"It's reminiscent," says Carter, "of the dark days of Communism when the church was forced to operate underground." But it is a tactful way to avoid further confrontation with the authorities. This night 464 people are baptised, and in the final session the following month, another 207 follow the example of Jesus in baptism.

In all, 3488 people are baptised, the largest baptism of Ukrainian people by any denomination in the 1000 years since Christianity gained its first foothold here. It is also believed to be the largest Adventist baptism in the world to this time.

After the Kiev meetings, the new Christians are organised into 24 new congregations. The Carter team hires public halls for them to hold their meetings. And they pay for the hall rentals 12 months in advance to reduce the financial burden on the new congregations. Weekly attendance records are kept at each church. If a new convert stops attending, someone is assigned to visit and encourage them in their Christian walk. Local church administrators report Carter's system to keep new converts in the church is the best of all overseas evangelists. Statistics for Carter's 15 years in the former USSR show *The Carter Report* has the highest retention rate of any evangelistic program. And here in Kiev, fewer new members will leave the church than for any of Carter's other series. In six months time, Carter will return to take revival meetings for the new converts. Then he will return every 12 months for the next six years.

Among those baptised in Kiev are all 70 members of a local symphony orchestra. They have all remained in the church and always perform whenever Carter visits.

Carter's converts are also evangelistically focused. He has not just taught them Bible doctrines and introduced them to the good news of salvation; he has imbued them with missionary zeal. Seven years after his Kiev campaign, the pastor of one Kiev Adventist church commented on this difference. "The best missionaries I have in my church are those baptised in the Carter meetings," he says.

Almost all the new converts are poor. It is impossible for them to build churches by themselves. Carter supporters and others helped finance a huge church building project for Kiev. Construction drags on for years because the locals are too poor to make up financial shortfalls when they occur. The building is eventually finished in 2004. The church seats 2400 people. It has the largest seating capacity of any Protestant church in Europe.

After the Kiev meetings, Carter produces a TV program about the series. The 30-minute video won six international TV awards.

However, as Jesus suggested, the real reward is in heaven: "Be happy when others insult you, persecute you, and falsely say great evil against you because of me. Rejoice and be glad because your reward will be great in heaven; for this is how they persecuted the prophets before you" (see Matthew 5:11, 12).

How John Carter came to Russia

S o who is this seemingly lone man who made such an impact on the formerly Communist world?

John Carter is the pastor of a medium-sized church in Los Angeles. He was born in Queensland, Australia, shortly before the start of World War II. He is married to Beverley. They have three adult children—all born in Australia—but who now live in California. They care about people, just like their parents.

David is their firstborn and only son. He works as a full-time TV producer for his father's weekly TV program. Leanne was born in Canberra and is a psychologist in San Francisco. Julilynn, born in Mackay, Queensland, is an intensive care nurse also in San Francisco.

John Carter trained as a minister and was ordained in 1967. He specialised in public evangelism and became one of Australia's leading Adventist evangelists. He was then called by the Adventist Church to be a pastor and evangelist in Fort Worth, Texas. There he ran two evangelistic campaigns that baptised 160 people. While in Texas he started a weekly religious TV program called *The Carter Report*.

In 1989, an Adventist offered the Adventist Church a million dollars to run an evangelistic campaign in Los Angeles. The president of the Southern California Conference of Seventh-day Adventists wanted to run the campaign, but had to find a suitable evangelist. He approached Carter in Texas and he agreed. The president then arranged to transfer Carter's employment to Los Angeles. He was to run the evangelistic campaign in the Shrine Auditorium and to be the pastor of the Hollywood Seventh-day Adventist church.

Carter was put to work organising the campaign. Intensive TV, radio, print and outdoor advertising created the largest opening attendance ever at an Adventist evangelistic series in the United States. The success continued as the series progressed. Responding to a specific appeal, 3500 people signed pledge cards to say they would keep the Sabbath they had learned about from the Bible.

But, unknown to Carter, there were some serious problems at the administrative level. First, the money hadn't yet arrived. Second, while the president had approved the project, he hadn't ratified it with his executive committee. And the committee didn't approve. The loose ends at management level proved too much, and the church administration told Carter to stop the meetings. This was a bitter disappointment for Carter, but it meant he was looking for new opportunities.

At that time the Adventist Church's administrative body, the General Conference, was contemplating evangelism in the USSR. They wanted to send a proven evangelist to Russia to test the waters. Because of Carter's unique situation, he had time available. He was sent to Russia and he proved it could be done.

Dozens of evangelists followed the path he blazed. But most of them had other duties and, after a year or two, did not return. Carter, on the other hand, had only limited duties in Los Angeles. So when the others stopped, he continued running campaigns in Russia and Ukraine.

To Chernobyl
with love

Beverley Carter is extremely concerned about orphans. Whenever her husband preaches in the former USSR, she visits the local orphanages. She finds out their needs and uses her considerable talents to make sure those needs are met.

"The saddest hospital I ever visited was one on the outskirts of Kiev," Beverley recalls. "It had children whose parents were victims of the Chernobyl disaster. They took me into a room and the stench was nearly overpowering. I don't know what the problem was, but they were not changing the babies' diapers [nappies]. There were 20 or 30 babies in that room and they were all being neglected. The babies had brain damage or heart defects. It was pretty hard to take."

Driven by the despair she encountered, Beverley starts to make things happen.

Her husband is also deeply concerned for victims of Chernobyl, history's worst nuclear accident. His evangelistic series in Kiev is nine years after things went horribly wrong at the reactor.

An Adventist pastor in Chernobyl has arranged two large buses to bring people from Chernobyl to the Carter program, 100 kilometres

(60 miles) away in Kiev. So every night, the Carters see the victims at the meetings.

Continuing radiation at Chernobyl has been slowly killing the people who live there. Carter is particularly concerned for the young Adventist minister who lives and works with these people. "You should leave," Carter tells the young pastor. "It's not good for your health."

"Are you asking me to forsake these people?" the young pastor replies.

"No, I'm not," Carter says.

And a huge degree of respect swells within his breast for the young shepherd who is literally giving his life for his sheep.

John and Beverley plan how they can help the victims of Chernobyl and others around Kiev. When they return to America, they raise the issue on *The Carter Report* TV program. An Adventist businessman, Dudley Snarr, phones to tell them about a company in Portland, Oregon, that often sells medical equipment to charities for 1 per cent of the true cost.

But Beverley's shopping list is not just for a few hundred dollars worth of gear. The equipment she wants is enough to fit out an entire hospital.

The amount of equipment she secures weighs more than 11 tonnes (25,000 pounds). It's wonderful to get this much equipment, but it could cost a fortune to transport it to Kiev.

Where can you get a plane big enough to carry that much—and without cost? Someone suggests asking the United States Air Force— "The worst they can say is no!" It's a daring move, but one that pays dividends. The US Air Force agrees to supply a Hercules transport plane to fly the medical supplies from Portland, USA, to Kiev.

Carter receives a phone call one day. "We've never flown to Kiev before. Can you arrange to get us permission to land?"

"I'm just a humble Seventh-day Adventist minister," he replies. "How could I get permission to land a US Air Force plane in Ukraine? If the United States Air Force can't arrange to land a plane, no-one can do it."

After some negotiation, the Hercules C-130 leaves the US, refuels in England and Germany, and within the hour it will land at Kiev International Airport. Carter stands at the head of a delegation ready to greet its arrival. The group includes the leaders of the Christian Adventist Church, the United States Ambassador and leaders of the government in Kiev. They all conveniently overlook the fact that six months ago government leaders were trying to run Carter out of town. Today he is a local hero. The political leaders are all very respectful and thankful to Carter.

It's a wet and cold afternoon. The official party is standing in an open area of the airport, well away from the commercial airline terminal. TV news crews and newspaper photographers stand a little away from the official party chatting to each other while they wait. The drivers of two 18-wheel trucks are sitting in their rigs to keep out of the cool breeze. Watching suspiciously are Ukrainian soldiers with their machine guns at the ready.

"There it is! There it is!" The Hercules has flown surprisingly close before the gathered dignitaries notice. It flies once over the airport, which gives TV cameramen an excellent view of the giant plane's underbelly. It circles around wide and low. And when it touches down, it seems to use just a short amount of the long Kiev runway.

This is the first time a plane from the US Air Force has landed in the independent Republic of Ukraine—and John and Beverley are the ones who have made it happen. The Hercules taxis to the corner of the airport where the dignitaries have gathered and lowers its rear loading ramp. The semitrailer that pulls up behind it looks like a dwarf. The Hercules is almost 30 metres (100 feet) long and 12 metres (40 feet) tall. The long cargo area is packed with medical supplies and equipment. Church members walk toward the plane to start unloading it.

The aircrew alights. There's 10 of them, including a woman. One of the aircrew is actually with the CIA because this is a big event in the politics of the day.

"Which one of you is John Carter?" they ask.

Ukrainian TV cameramen weave in and out of the group. There is the occasional camera flash. Officials stand in line for photos. While the attitudes of the Cold War are vanishing, this will only be a brief stop—just long enough to unload the cargo and say a few words. They are allowed only half-an-hour and then the plane must leave.

"You were here six months ago conducting evangelistic meetings. You have returned with a giant plane packed with medical supplies. Why are you doing this?" a television reporter asks Carter.

"Christian Adventists don't just believe in preaching and teaching," he replies. "It's part of our religion to help the poor, the sick and the oppressed. Jesus did this. And we must do it too."

This is a happy half-hour for Carter. But it's an even more emotional time for these members of the US Air Force. This is not just another assignment. This is breaking Cold War ice. One of them rips a "US Air Force" emblem off his uniform and gives it to a Ukrainian. Another crew member does the same. Dozens of Ukrainians receive emblems from the aircrew.

The customs officers place seals on the closed doors of the two semitrailers, which then drive away.

"It sure beats dropping bombs, doesn't it!" the pilot comments to Carter before he climbs back on board. The Hercules propellers whirl. The plane moves slowly to the runway, and then gets clearance for take-off. The dignitaries watch until it is just a dot on its way to Germany, then they walk to their vehicles.

The aircrew and the dignitaries feel it's been a significant day for international relations. But more importantly for John and Beverley, it's a significant day for the victims of Chernobyl.

CRISIS IN
ST PETERSBURG

Educated people often feel less need of God. Their greater learning and opportunity allows them to earn more money and achieve higher status in society. They tend to draw their security from their wealth and position, rather than depending on God.

Even the New Testament writer Paul noticed this. He wrote: "My friends, remember what you were like when you were called. Not many of you were wise, influential or well bred by earthly standards" (see 1 Corinthians 1:26).

This trend makes the baptisms at the Carter program in St Petersburg particularly remarkable: 80 per cent of those baptised were college or university graduates.

St Petersburg—called Leningrad in the Communist era—was always different from other Russian cities. Tsar Peter the Great built it in 1703 to be a "window to Europe" and, from its first days, the city reflected European values. Three hundred years later, it is still the most "European" of any Russian city. St Petersburg is outward looking and progressive.

Today, with a population of almost five million, it is Russia's second largest city and Europe's fourth largest city. Near the Arctic Circle, for three months of the year the midnight sun is only just below the horizon, giving the city its famous "white nights."

St Petersburg has stunning architecture. It has numerous canals with granite embankments, vast open spaces, parks and gardens, monuments and world-famous sculptures. Nine drawbridges span the Neva River. The city has 22 royal palaces and hundreds of stonework bridges built with superb masonry. A renowned cultural centre, it is full of universities, theatres and museums. The entire city centre is included on the World Heritage List.

Carter has taken a year to raise the money for his 1997 series in St Petersburg. The indoor stadium he is using seats 15,000 people. It is the largest venue he will ever book in the former USSR. Perhaps the team were intimidated by the size of the venue, because they planned only two sessions on the opening Saturday. They filled the stadium for both sessions and 10,000 people were turned away. Reflecting on this experience, Carter says if he were doing it again, he would have plans for an unadvertised extra session should more people come than expected.

The three words Carter uses to describe the St Petersburg audience are "serious, suspicious and intellectual." But there is also a strong spiritual hunger. Looking down to the front row, he sees a person in a wheelchair—a man who brings himself 24 kilometres (15 miles) to the meetings each night in his wheelchair.

A group of Adventist musicians from Columbia Union College—The New England Youth Ensemble—performs at each program of the first week. It proves a good match for the culture of the city. "The audience is every bit as sophisticated as New York City," Carter remembers.

In St Petersburg, Carter's program appeals to both educated and uneducated. He speaks in short sentences, especially when speaking though a translator, making it easy for poorly educated people to understand him.

But the thoughts he expresses are not shallow. The depth of the material he presents appeals to the educated people in his audience. He describes his programs as "meat for the intellectuals, nourishment for the uneducated."

One Russian general summarised Carter's meetings in this way: "You are giving us facts. You are not like the priests. We are hearing science."

Carter strongly believes Christians are saved by faith. But the first week of his meetings presents logical reasons for that faith, logical reasons to believe the Bible. He tells a team meeting, "It's my belief that faith is based on evidence."

The evidence Carter presents on the opening night in St Petersburg is from ancient history. The presentation shows about 100 photos of Egypt on the stadium's giant screens. He tells little-known facts about ancient Egyptian culture. He tells them about "the bearded queen," Hatshepsut. He gives evidence suggesting she was the foster-mother of Moses. The audience sees an astonishing link between ancient history and the Bible, supporting its historical accuracy.

On the second night, Carter's program looks at how astronomy reveals a Creator. He talks about four critical forces needed in balance at the time of the "big bang." Mathematically, he says, there is only one chance in 1,000,000,000,000,000 of those four elements happening at once. "So it is fanciful to think the universe created itself," he tells the St Petersburg audience. "It is beyond the laws of mathematical probability. It is, therefore, far-fetched to believe that the universe created itself.

"Alan Sandage is one of the world's greatest cosmologists," Carter tells the audience. "He was an atheist until he did the mathematics. Then one day at Berkeley University, he made a major announcement. He said he could no longer believe the universe came into existence without the power of God."

Carter's presentation stuns the honest atheists in the audience. They are deeply impressed by the force of his logic. His 90-minute presentation is so astonishing almost every atheist in the audience returns the next night.

For the first week of his program, he has the audience lights off so they can see the pictures on the screen. From the eighth night, he stops showing pictures and has the hall lights turned up full. But in academic St Petersburg in the first few days, people want to take detailed notes of what he is saying. Scattered through the stadium are dozens of people with torches shining on notepads. They are writing down all Carter is saying.

The third night's program is how prophecy provides evidence about God. The church members who work as the program's ushers have 30,000 Bibles at the St Petersburg Palace of Sport. They give one Bible to each person in the vast audience.

Carter opens his Bible to Daniel 2 and he encourages the audience to open to the same page. He reads verses to them about a statue made of various metals. The audience uses the Bibles they hold to follow the passages he reads aloud. During the presentation he writes key words on a giant blackboard: *Babylon, Media-Persia, Greece, Rome, Divided Europe.*

These empires are represented by the metals in the Daniel 2 statue, Carter tells his amazed audience. "How could a human being writing in Nebuchadnezzar's Babylon so accurately predict the history of the world?" he asks. "Only *God* could know these things before they happened!" he declares.

He then turns in his Bible to a prediction about the ancient city of Tyre. "In its day," he tells the audience, "Tyre was the greatest seaport in the world." A succession of photos of the site of this ancient city appears on the screen behind him. He tells how the Babylonians besieged Tyre for 12 years. The St Petersburg audience understands the suffering of a siege; their city was besieged by the Germans in World War II.

The audience is asked to open their Bibles to Ezekiel 26:4: "They shall destroy Tyre's walls and break down its towers. I will scrape its soil from it and make it a bare rock."

Carter explains how the Babylonians—and then the army of Alexander the Great—fulfilled this prophecy. You could hear a pin drop in this vast auditorium. The audience is astounded that the Bible accurately predicted such an unusual occurrence. Throwing the destroyed city of Tyre's stones and soil into the sea! It's astonishing. But he has even more in store for them.

He turns his Bible to verses about Memphis, once the capital city of Egypt. He reads Jeremiah 46:19: "Memphis shall be laid waste and lie in ruins without inhabitants." Behind him, the screen shows pictures of the date palms growing where the great city once stood. The photos show the site—now uninhabited—just as the Bible predicted. Again the audience sees that the predictions of the Bible they hold in their hands have been proved true.

Carter has four giant blackboards on the stage. Each night before the program begins, he and his translator write key summary points on the board. Before the meetings start in this academic city, about

100 people come down to the stage and copy the blackboard points into their notebooks. And after the meeting, another 20 or 30 people also come to the stage to write down the key points.

The next night's program, with the intriguing title "The man who wrote his own life story before he was born," explores Bible predictions about Jesus written hundreds of years before His birth. Then he explains that Jesus gave His life for us. Tears of joy roll down hundreds of faces.

✳ ✳ ✳

St Petersburg is a very liberal city. The Carter program receives no threats from the government here. There's no opposition from other churches and the program continues smoothly. At last, it seems a Carter program will run in Russia without anything major going wrong. But at the end of the second week, Carter is hit with serious illness.

He is rushed by ambulance to a public hospital. His wife and son go with him. His blood pressure is dangerously high. Medication lowers the blood pressure and all seems well. His family leaves and a young woman Carter had baptised stays to sleep in the hall outside his room. She speaks English and Russian, so she can translate for him.

On the second night in hospital he receives a medication overdose. His blood pressure drops life-threateningly low. The doctor on the night shift is drunk. There are no bedside phones to ring out for help. The intoxicated doctor comes with a needle but Carter will not let him use it. So the doctor goes back to his vodka and doesn't check on his patient again for the rest of the night.

"Julia," Carter calls to his Russian carer. "They will kill me here. Go and find a phone. Call my family and the team. Let them know what's happening."

Julia searches the hospital for a phone, but the office is locked. On the street at 2 am, she cannot find a phone, but she does find a taxi. Half-an-hour later she arrives at the hotel, and wakes Beverley and David. At about 3.30 they arrive at the hospital.

Meanwhile, Carter knows he could die from his induced low blood pressure. He decides to get out of bed and exercise to raise his blood pressure. The nurses try to stop him, but he pushes his way out of bed.

Carter's family arrives, fearing they might find him dead. Instead, they find him jogging along a hospital corridor trying to raise his blood pressure. As soon as it is light, they transfer him to the American Clinic in the city. His health insurance covers emergency evacuations, so he is evacuated by air to the United States.

"I must admit there were a few scary moments," Carter said recalling the incident a few years later. "In fact, it was the most dramatic time of my life. But through it all I felt the calming influence of the One who said, 'I will never leave you or forsake you' [Hebrews 13:5]. During those dark days the words of the Bible were my consoling companion. I particularly remembered the words of the twenty-third psalm, 'Though I walk through the valley of the shadow of death, I will fear no evil.' This brought me hope and comfort."

Carter and his translator always have a detailed rehearsal before each day's program. Carter tells him exactly what he plans to do on the stage. They go through the sermon so the translator will know all the key concepts and know the Russian words for any obscure English words Carter plans to use. The translator knows exactly what to do so he can mimic Carter's preaching.

But with Carter in hospital, the translator is now on his own. If the translator had worked with him in previous years, he would have been well acquainted with his material. However, Carter has a new translator working with him this year. The young translator goes to Carter's hotel room to get his notes for the evening meeting. He holds a rehearsal by himself. And then 21-year-old Vadim (pronounced *Verdeem*) Butov walks out in front of 12,000 people who are expecting to see 59-year-old John Carter.

This is a "make or break" moment for the future of the program—and for the future of the church in St Petersburg. Some people become attached to a preacher. Many in the stadium tonight may not come back if they don't like the translator's solo presentation.

But the translator has mimicked Carter for the past 10 nights. When the translator takes over the St Petersburg meetings, Carter's presence is still felt on the stage. The attendance losses are minimal. And in the next few weeks, 1000 people will be baptised.

Carter had scheduled a 28-night program, so Vadim has to speak alone for 18 nights. This task is more difficult than it would appear. When Carter takes an hour program in Russia, he talks for only half-an-hour, with the translator talking for the other half-hour. Now Vadim is doing *all* the talking, Carter's notes will give him only a 30-minute meeting. How will he fill in the extra time?

He picks up an idea Carter has used on one or two nights and decides to run it in every program. He has a 15-minute question-and-answer period each night. This works especially well with the intellectual St Petersburg audience and warms them up for the sermon. Fortunately, Vadim knows his Bible well. He doesn't answer the audience questions with his own opinion. He opens his Bible to read the answer. And usually, he has the audience open their Bibles so they can read it also. The young translator is able to show the Bible's answer for everything these intellectuals ask.

Vadim comes through with flying colours. No-one could have guessed it when the series began. Then he was just another aspiring 21-year-old minister. But his incredible work at St Petersburg put him on the path to become one of Russia's most successful home-grown evangelists. "St Petersburg was a great evangelistic university for me," he later said.

Had a lesser person taken over from Carter, the St Petersburg project could have been a disaster. But not only did that program succeed, it was the making of another great evangelist. In the next nine years, Vadim will run 47 evangelistic campaigns and plant 31 new churches.

There were two Christian Adventist churches in St Petersburg before the Carter–Butov program began. When the program ends, six more congregations are formed to care for the 1000 new believers.

ON THE TRANS-SIBERIAN EXPRESS

The Trans-Siberian Express runs on the world's longest regular railway, a journey of more than 9250 kilometres (5750 miles). It leaves Moscow at midnight and rushes east through spectacular scenery for eight days. It crosses eight time zones and runs a third of the way around the globe.

Building the railway was the world's biggest engineering project of the 19th century. It consumed two-thirds of Russia's annual budget. In real terms, construction cost twice as much as putting man on the moon. When completed, it was three times longer than any railway of its day.

For much of the 100 years since, the Trans-Siberian Express has been a magnet, drawing travellers from all over the world. Now John Carter is at a Moscow railway station about to board the train. But his reasons for travel on this most famous express are different from any of the millions of travellers before him.

A few months earlier, Carter's Russian translator had shared a deep concern. He had seen the gospel booming for five years in Ukraine and in western Russia. But his heart was breaking for the people of Russia's far-flung eastern provinces. Carter and the translator discussed it and hatched an idea that eventually led them to gather tonight on this Moscow railway station.

A team of 10 Adventists farewell their friends and step aboard the legendary train. They have hired its entire last carriage. This is normally luxury accommodation. But their trip will be anything but comfortable, especially over the first part of the journey. Each cabin of the carriage is packed from floor to ceiling with dozens of boxes, with barely enough room for any of them to sleep.

Their project is to deliver Bibles, religious audiotapes, medicines, vitamins and encouragement at the railway stations in Siberia. Church members live in most towns along the railway line. Some churches in these towns were started by deliberate evangelism. Others started when Christian Adventists moved there and shared their faith. Yet others started when Adventists, who were jailed in Siberia for their religious beliefs, continued to spread those beliefs when released from prison.

Church members at each town on the rail line have been alerted to meet the train at whatever time it comes in—midnight, 3 am, midday, whenever. At most stations the stay will be less than 15 minutes. But enough time for a blessing, a brief message of encouragement and a short prayer.

The church members in this string of remote cities are excited. They will meet John Carter, who in the past five years has become a household name for Adventists in Russia. They'll also meet a senior official in their church, Pastor Alexander Antonyuk, the president of the Volgo-Vyatskaya Conference of the Adventist Church.

The team will give them medicines and vitamins to compensate for their inadequate diets—estimates at this time suggest 40 per cent of the population suffers from malnutrition and 60 per cent have vitamin deficiencies.

They will receive sets of audio recordings of a complete 24-sermon Carter evangelistic series. And they'll carry away boxloads of precious Russian Bibles to use themselves or to share with their friends and neighbours.

In every city where there is a Christian Adventist church nearby, people attend these trackside meetings. But for those in the last carriage, it is disappointing to see so many towns without church spires, which would indicate a Christian presence.

Carter's team is making the journey in midwinter. They feel this is the time when church members will most appreciate this uplift. The midwinter cold is when life is at its worst in Siberia. And it turns out the Carter team has judged their timing well. Church members express their delight that their leaders have come to visit them in midwinter.

Pastor Bj (Bjarne) Christensen, the president of the Adventist Church in Southern California, is keeping the project organised. He knows the size of each local church along the line. And before the train pulls in, he has the appropriate materials stacked beside the doors ready to unload. The quicker the boxes are unloaded, the more time the members will have for the revival meeting that follows.

The project operates like clockwork with hardly anything going wrong. The team even has its own set of floodlights. When the train pulls into a stopping place at night, they connect these lights to the carriage's electrical system. Then they have plenty of light for their time with their brothers and sisters in faith. "Where else in the world can you hold an evangelistic meeting at midnight?" Carter comments to the team.

The whole world knows that life in Siberia was bitter during the Communist era. But in the six years since Communism ended, life for many people is even worse. The government has run out of money to pay the wages of public servants and pensions to the elderly. Many people along the railway line haven't had income for months. They are desperate for anything that will help them avoid starvation. This is the desperate situation as the train rolls into station after station.

In midafternoon on a sunny but bitterly cold winter day, the train slows as it approaches a city called Nazivayevskay. An aged Russian grandmother walks across the snow to where the train will stop. She wears a white scarf pulled tightly over her head and a thick grey overcoat the colour of her ageing hair. She has blue eyes and a gentle face. She wears no make-up but because the temperature is minus 26°C (-15°F), the cold colours her cheeks and lips. Despite the wrinkles of age, she has one of the prettiest faces you could imagine.

She carries three giant sausages, about a week's ration of food. She needs cash and wants to sell the sausages to passengers on the train when it makes its 15-minute stop.

The Carter team alights and commence their meeting with a group of waiting church members. The woman with blue eyes is curious. She hears a Westerner speaking to the group. Perhaps the Westerner will buy her sausages?

As the woman nears the group, she sees Carter is giving Russian Bibles to the church members. The woman sees the Bibles and changes her mind. She no longer wants cash; she wants a Bible. She has no money; however, she does have sausages. She approaches

Carter and through the translator she tells him she will give him three sausages in return for a Bible. But he will not accept her sausages.

"This is God's Word," Carter tells the blue-eyed woman through the translator. "It is our gift to you. It comes to you with our love. It is free. It tells the story of a great Creator God who gave His only Son so you may have eternal life."

A gentle smile creeps across the woman's face. She accepts the gift and leaves, taking her new Russian Bible with her. The Carter team members have no way of knowing what good that Bible will do. But the woman's smile suggests that giving her the Scriptures was the right thing to do.

The train rumbles on. They herald each stop with a trumpet call. One of the team (the late Dr Boris Belko, whose ancestors were Russian) has a trumpet, and as the train is stopping he leans out the window, with strong arms preventing him from falling. And he plays the tune "Lift up the trumpet, and loud let it ring: Jesus is coming again!" Those gathered at each station have no doubt something different is happening at today's train.

The Carter team gives a Bible, a bottle of vitamins, headache tablets for fever and 12 religious audiotapes to every church member living along the line. For many of these people it means a journey of hours for them to meet the train. Many of the people who come to meet the Carters have never before seen a Westerner. John Carter preaches a brief revival message. And despite the cold, the group sings Christian songs vigorously, even at three in the morning—even at minus 37°C (-35°F).

Every few hours in town after town, the trumpet calls the faithful to gather. But in one town the melody gives way to a terrible trumpet sound. It is so cold the trumpet mouthpiece has frozen to the player's mouth. He has to carefully pry it off, without pulling his lips off in the process.

In one city the church members have hired a bus. Their church is 100 kilometres (60 miles) from the railway station. Since most of them don't have cars, the bus takes them to the train. The church members arrive two hours before the train is due and wait expectantly. The train pulls in. But there doesn't seem to be anything special about the last carriage. No-one gets out. No-one greets them. There are no Bibles, no vitamins, no prayers and no singing. The church members are deeply disappointed as the train pulls out. They return to their homes without explanation.

However, the pastor stays at the station wondering if perhaps the blessing will come with tomorrow's train. It is 26 hours since he began waiting when the next train rolls in. But he is rewarded for his faithfulness.

Carter jumps from the carriage onto the snow, and walks toward this man standing alone with his arms folded.

"*Adventista?*" Carter asks. And the pastor's face lights up.

The team gives the pastor the gifts for each of his church members.

The one-person welcoming committee at this station is the smallest group of church members who meet the train. In most locations, between 20 and 100 people are waiting at the station. The largest group is 200.

Carter wants his message heard by more than just the assembled Christians. His powerful voice can be heard by the largest group that gathers beside the carriage. But he wants his message heard further away than that. When the team alights from the train at each stop, several of them quickly connect a public-address system to the carriage's power outlet. And when he starts preaching, people can hear it almost a kilometre (half a mile) away.

"You are not a machine. You are not an animal. You are a child of God. We have come here today to tell you that God loves you. You are not forgotten," Carter proclaims urgently. And thousands of people who cannot see what's happening hear the Christian message.

Carter's signal to stop preaching is when the train whistle blows, meaning they have only two minutes before the express will pull out. At that point the team breaks into its regular pattern, with everyone doing their allocated task. The floodlights and the public-address system are disconnected from the carriage's power supply. They are packed and placed on the train. It is an efficient system, although a few times the timing isn't quite perfect and some team members have to jump on the moving train.

The express comes to one town where there is no church, so there are no church members to meet them. But rather than stay in the carriage, some team members jump out into the snow to enjoy themselves. There is a clear blue sky, but it's minus 40°. And although it is two in the afternoon, it is not long before sunset.

Pastor Antonyuk decides to prove what a tough man he is. He pulls off his shirt, throws it into the carriage, and starts rubbing the bitterly cold snow on his chest. Not to be outdone, Carter's translator, Pastor Igor Pospehin, does the same. Then they start rubbing snow on each other. Next the two strong men lift Carter above their heads as a "musclemen" stunt. Everyone is laughing and enjoying this unique brand of Russian humour. Perhaps the laughter drowns out the train whistle.

The train starts to move and the "strong men" run toward the carriage carrying Carter. They push him onto the train and he barely makes it. As the train gathers speed, the "strong men" run as fast as they can to catch it. Arms reaching out of the carriage grab hold of Alexander and drag him aboard. For a moment, it seems they will not be able to take hold of the translator. But he makes one more desperate effort and is grabbed by his fingertips.

It would have been most unpleasant if the "strong men" had missed the train and been left in the middle of Siberia, half-naked, with no money and a bitterly cold night about to descend. There is no church in the town, and often in places like this Christians are the only ones who will help a stranger in need.

Beverley Carter's heart is particularly touched at one station. A group of children come and stand close to the train. Some are very dirty urchins.

"What are they doing?" Beverley asks the Russian stewardess in charge of their carriage.

"They come every day," the stewardess replies. "They stand here to get warmth from the heat of the train. Some of them are orphans. Some of their parents are alcoholics. I give them leftover food that the passengers have not eaten."

Beverley returns to the carriage and gathers as much fresh bread as she can. Just before the train departs, she gives it to the children. The train pulls out with Beverley's heart saddened that she cannot do any more. But the children are happy: their next meal will be much better than leftovers.

The train is now approaching Irkutsk. Here their special carriage is disconnected from the express and shunted into a siding. They are staying for a whole day at Irkutsk. John Carter is scheduled to hold an evangelistic campaign in this Siberian city in six months time. The extra day will give him time to get a feeling for the town. There is a strong church here and about 200 believers meet the train when it arrives—the largest group to meet the team on their journey. They have a wonderful time of fellowship, which continues well into the night.

Siberia is notorious for its prisons and in the morning Carter goes to visit one. During the 70 years of Communism, an average of a million people a year were sent to Siberia's concentration camps. Ten million of them died in prison. It is now six years since the fall of Communism, but a million prisoners are still in the jails here. Many are dying from tuberculosis spread from prisoner to prisoner, transforming a short jail term into a death sentence. Almost nothing is being done to stop this fatal lung disease spreading among the prisoners. However, the Carter team members want to do something about it.

An Adventist who works in a prison had sent Carter a message: "We desperately need your help. Bring Bibles and medicines for the prisoners. The doors are open to you. The prison officials will welcome you."

Carter takes boxes full of Bibles to the prison. His heart bleeds for the prisoners. They too are children of God, and he thinks what he has done to help them has not been enough. He wants to do more—something that will provide benefit long after he has gone.

"Behind me is a Russian work-camp," Carter says, recording an impromptu segment for his American TV audience. "In these work-camps in the days of the Communists, prisoners went through hell. They were brutalised and finally put to death. However, conditions in these concentration camps today are no better than they were in the days of Stalin. The prisoners are still brutalised. Many of them are suffering from tuberculosis. Just a few days ago I received a message from one of the people who works inside one of these prisons." He relates the message he has received.

The prison is poorly maintained, as its crumbling red-and-white, clay-brick walls testify. The walls are topped with the usual coils of razor wire. Above is a grey sky, with snow on the ground all around. It is set in a truly desolate landscape.

Standing in front of these walls, Carter holds a microphone in gloves half the size of basketballs and ends his appeal to the TV audience. "Please stand with us in this great work of bringing hope to the prisoners. Write to me and help us to bring hope to the people here in Siberia. This is John Carter reporting from Siberia."

The camera stops rolling. He wraps up the microphone cable and helps carry video equipment back to the carriage in the siding. Within a few months the message he has recorded will bring hope and salvation to inmates helplessly locked up in Siberia's prisons.

The Trans-Siberian moves on. On average it is about two or three hours between stations. The express makes 91 stops in eight days. Throughout the journey they have constantly disturbed sleep. They take off their heavy clothing, go to bed and go to sleep. But they seem to have only just started to doze when Christensen pulls each person's feet to let them know it is 10 minutes to the next stop. So, after barely getting to sleep they must wake again, put on their heavy clothes and go out to meet the people. Carter never shirks his duty. At every stop where Christians have gathered, he wakes up to share the gospel with them.

While the teams spend little time actually with the people, they feel like they are working 20-hour days. They are not getting any significant amounts of uninterrupted sleep. Their bodies experience the confusion that long-distance train travellers often report. They reset their watches each day as they cross into another time zone. But it is hard to discipline their appetites to eat at the right time in each day's new time zone.

Sometimes the train stops at a station for half-an-hour, giving the team a reasonable time to fellowship with the local church members. Sometimes the stop is only three minutes, barely enough time to offload their boxes and have a brief word with the church members. But, whether the stops are long or short, they are a blessing.

The church members realise they are not alone. The leaders of their church are interested in them and have shown it by travelling a great distance to briefly pray with them. And from these simple human actions these isolated Christians are reminded that Heaven itself is interested in their efforts to live the Christian faith in their difficult circumstances. They are not alone—that's the message of these whistle-stop prayer meetings

Over the journey, the team delivers 6000 bottles of vitamin pills, 72,000 audiotapes of Carter's meetings, 6000 bottles of aspirin plus other medicines and 6000 Bibles—all in a journey of 9250 kilometres (5750 miles).

June 1999

AT GUNPOINT IN
SIBERIA

John Carter goes into the hotel room of his son, David. He greets Dave and a young man named Costa, who works as a translator. Carter turns to close the door. Suddenly six men burst into the room with pistols and submachine guns!

They use the muzzles of their guns to threaten the Carters. They mean business.

The six men are extremely agitated. They keep waving their guns in a most threatening manner.

They are wearing ski-masks on their heads to hide their identities and, though the room is small, they're shouting at the top of their voices. But John and David cannot understand a word.

As soon as the men burst in, David shouted to the young translator, "What are they saying? Tell us! What are they saying?" But the 22-year-old is too terrified to speak. He believes they are going to die.

The Carters can't find out what these six men are demanding. And the longer the stand-off lasts, the more angry the men become.

The gunmen are acting as if it's a life-and-death matter for them. And it certainly feels like it's life and death to the Carters.

They respond to the Russian shouting by shouting back in English. "We're Australians! We're Australians!" But it seems to make no difference. The Russians just keep shouting. But in hindsight, David believes it may have saved their lives. "If we were Russians, I suppose we would have had a bullet in our heads," he said recalling the ordeal.

The hotel room is small, with space for one bed and almost nothing else. But now nine people are crammed into the room. There's only a small space between the men waving the guns and the victims they're trying to terrorise. The room is full of confusion, and any slip could mean death.

Patrons in the other rooms can hear what's happening—but none of them dares do anything to help. In Russia, even today, force speaks louder than words.

The guns have raised Carter's adrenaline level, but not his fear level. And the longer the threatening continues, the greater his confidence grows.

Soon David realises the problem is a videotape. He is in Siberia working on the technical side of his father's evangelistic campaign. A few minutes earlier there had been a drug bust at their hotel. As the Russian Special Security Forces were making their raid, David took video of it through his hotel window.

After five minutes of shouting in Russian, one of the masked men stammers a few words in broken English. And now Costa, the Carters' translator, starts talking too.

The masked men are police, members of the Special Security Force. When they carry out their drug raids, they cover their faces. Although their faces were covered in this raid, if a drug lord saw the videotape, some of them may be recognised. The police believe the

Carters were taking video for the drug lords.

It's now easy for John and David to understand the desperation of these six. They are trying to save their own lives.

But John feels this tape is his property. They have no right to take it. Besides, he's already thinking how he can use it for his television program. And the tape also has video on it of that night's meeting. So he refuses to give them the tape. It is a stubborn streak that often wins him the battle. He doesn't seem worried that the masked men may kill them to get the tape.

David has a different idea of the tape's value. He doesn't believe it's worth dying for. He feels nothing he videoed through the hotel window has any value. He cannot sell it to television news because it's just one of hundreds of drug raids. And he doesn't think it would be significant footage in a *Carter Report* TV program.

"Don't get us killed," David says to his father.

With John Carter stubbornly on one side and the masked men desperate on the other, David comes up with a compromise. He will erase the videotape in the masked men's presence. His father will keep the tape itself. But the masked men won't have to worry about being recognised.

Despite the pressure of a machine gun at close range, David is surprised to realise he is thinking clearly. David has his work cut out to convince both his father and the masked men to accept his idea. But at least he has a workable plan.

Everything in Russia takes three times longer than it does in the West. Russians want a committee meeting to make almost every decision. And these masked men are no different. Cramped in that very small hotel room, they hold a committee meeting.

John Carter is now gaining in confidence, giving even stronger replies to what they say. From David's point of view, it's getting tougher. However, it's almost developed into a game to John, who is no longer treating it with total seriousness. Yet even at this stage, one slip of the trigger and someone could be dead.

The whole episode takes about 30 minutes. Eventually the committee of six faceless men reaches their decision. And Carter also agrees with his son's proposal.

Using video equipment in the room, David erases the tape. Six sets of watchful eyes carefully witness what happens. He then plays the tape back to the masked men to satisfy them the images are gone. Their leader double-checks. Then he is convinced. The crisis is over.

The six masked men disappear into the night.

A MISSION TO KILL JOHN CARTER

A young man carefully loads his pistol. He hides it under his coat and makes his way to an open-air sports stadium. His mission tonight is to kill John Carter. The young man weaves his way through the large audience to the front row.

Beverley Carter is on the stage talking. John isn't yet on stage. The assassin pauses at the front row, waiting for his victim to appear.

Standing out of sight, John Carter listens to what his wife is saying. She has almost finished her talk. He walks to the edge of the platform, ready to move onto the stage when Beverley finishes. Now Carter is visible. This is the moment the assassin's been waiting for.

Out of the corner of her eye, Beverley sees a young man with a gun jumping onto the stage. A thousand thoughts cross her mind at once: *Should I stop talking? Should I run? What will the crowd do if I show any sign of panic? Could people in the audience stampede and trample others to death?*

In an instant, Beverley decides to keep talking so the crowd won't panic. She and her translator are sharing the stage with an armed gunman. But she keeps talking as if the gunman weren't there.

The gunman moves across the stage toward her husband. *The Carter Report*'s bodyguard sees what's unfolding. He rushes forward to intercept the killer.

The bodyguard is a black belt in aikido (a Japanese martial art). So it should take only moments to put the gunman on the ground. Unexpectedly, he meets a gunman who is a black belt in karate. A vicious fight breaks out in full view of the audience. It's only brief, probably about 30 seconds, but it's brutal. This is the real thing, not a staged karate exhibition. And through it all, Beverley calmly keeps chatting to the audience so they will not panic.

The fighting gunman and bodyguard move off stage and continue to fight behind the curtain. Police who are standing around the edge of the stadium crowd run to the stage and into the fight. The gunman is subdued.

In all this time, the man didn't discharge a single bullet.

Beverley finishes her ad lib, and belatedly introduces her husband. She walks off the stage and John begins his scheduled presentation. Only then does Beverley become conscious of what she has done. Her calmness under pressure has saved a possible disaster.

Beverley moves to the place behind the curtain where she normally prays during her husband's meetings. But she has a special reason to pray tonight. "Thank you, God, that my husband was not killed," she breathes.

Behind the stage the bodyguard turns the gunman over to the local police. The police start bashing him. But it's only a brutal facade. The police know the man they are beating up is one of their own. But they keep bashing him to mislead the Carter team members who are watching.

The police then take the gunman away. But once they think

they're out of sight they set the gunman free. One member of the Carter team has followed at a distance. He sees the police release the gunman.

After the evening meeting, John and his son, David, talk to the police. When the police find out the Carters know they have released the gunman, they come clean. They admit they know the would-be assassin. He's a member of the Russian Special Security Forces. In fact, he is one of those involved in that drug raid at the Carter's hotel a few days before.

This is a worrying situation. John Carter decides to take the matter to the top. He demands answers.

Two days later senior officers of Russia's Special Security Forces meet with John and Beverley. A translator conveys their words. "We have come to apologise on behalf of the Russian Government. This man is one of our men. On his day off, he got drunk. He heard about your meetings and wanted to come down and question you. We are going to dishonourably discharge him and put him in prison for many years."

"I want to thank you for coming to see me and I accept your apology," Carter replies. "But I want to make a request of you."

"What is that?"

"As you know, I am a minister of the gospel," Carter explains. "If this young man goes to prison, it will be a death sentence because the prisons are full of tuberculosis."

"Yes, we know that," they reply.

"Here is my request. I have forgiven this young man for what he has done. And I'm asking you now to forgive him too. This is what the teachings of Christ tell us to do."

"This is amazing!" they exclaim. "Do you really mean this?"

"Yes, I do," says Carter. "Will you do this?"

"If you have forgiven him, then we will forgive him too," they respond.

The Carters then ask for a favour. "We would like some guards to protect us," they say.

The most senior officer then speaks. "We will do that. We will talk to this young man and tell him that he is forgiven. Then we will tell him he is appointed by us to attend all the meetings and serve as your personal bodyguard."

The officers are true to their word. Each night the young man stands there in his jet-black uniform. There is a bulge under his coat, presumably a loaded pistol. On his first night, he avoids talking to Carter. But after several nights he approaches the evangelist. "I wish to speak to you," he says. "I am very sorry. I was foolish. I was very drunk. It will never happen again. I will now protect you with my life."

Carter hugs him, as one good Russian does to another.

The meetings continue. At the end of one of them, Carter makes an appeal. He wants people to commit their lives to God. He asks the audience to raise their hands as a sign of that commitment. Many hands rise. Most of these are people he does not know. But he recognises one of the people making the commitment. A hand in a jet-black uniform is raised. It's the would-be assassin committing his life to God.

IN THE OPEN AIR

John Carter's first evangelistic campaign outside his homeland was in Papua New Guinea in 1981. In that South Pacific nation just north of Australia, he spoke to almost 10,000 people each night. The meetings were in the open air with Carter speaking from a stage set up on a football field. It was at that time the highest-ever attendance at any type of public meeting in the country's history. The meetings were broadcast on Papua New Guinea's only TV channel. They made a huge impact right across the nation. Carter was even invited to the residence of Prime Minister Sir Julias Chan, where he was given a ceremonial spear and made an honorary chief.

Now, 18 years later, he has booked another outdoor venue. But this one will not be in a tropical paradise, where even the rain is warm. These outdoor meetings will be in Siberia, with cold winds direct from the Arctic. The contrast between the two outdoor venues could not be greater.

Irkutsk is the main city of Siberia, with a population of 600,000. The city has tree-lined boulevards and stately old mansions and is sometimes called "the Paris of Siberia." It's located 60 kilometres (40 miles) from the beautiful Lake Baykal. This giant lake is 1.5 kilometres (one mile) deep and contains 20 per cent of the earth's fresh surface water. In winter the lake freezes so hard it is possible to drive a semitrailer across it.

Winters are long in Irkutsk and temperatures drop to minus 45°C (-50°F). Summers are short, but with temperatures sometimes climbing past 40°C (100°F). But summer temperatures can fluctuate greatly, depending whether the wind is from the ice-bound north or the hot deserts to the south.

Many of the citizens of Irkutsk are descendants of people exiled to Siberia. It wasn't just Stalin and Khrushchev who sent political prisoners here. The city has been a dumping ground for exiles since the 17th century. In the era of the Tsars, many artists, nobles, military officers and free thinkers were exiled here. In fact, in the era of the Tsars, Stalin himself was once exiled here.

This is both a cultural city and a tough town. The Mafia is active here.

There is little religion of any type. Before the Carter team arrived, there were only 120 Christian Adventist members in the city.

Having the meetings in the open air creates an unusual problem. The city is so close to the North Pole they have the famous "white nights." The sky at night doesn't go black in summer, meaning it is too light to run projectors. Photographic slides are normally the main part of the first seven days of a Carter program, so the first week of the program here must be different.

An open-air sports stadium is the only place large enough here for an evangelistic campaign. Unfortunately, the opening night has bitterly cold winds from the north. It is so cold the New England Youth Ensemble can barely move their fingers to play their music. Yet 13,000 people still come to the open-air meetings.

"This is not an easy audience to talk to," Carter comments after the opening meeting. In every other Russian or Ukrainian city, his audiences have listened quietly, attentively and respectfully. Here young people are drinking beer, smoking, talking and walking around the stadium while he speaks. He feels many people in this first-night audience are only half-listening.

The locals were so keen to get the famous John Carter to their town they stretched the truth a little. They said the population was a million—but the city is only a little more than half that size. And they said this month is the city's driest time of year. However, any encyclopedia will show it's the city's wettest month.

On the third night of his meetings, the temperature suddenly drops, thunder roars, and the crowd is drenched by rain. Carter has a canvas canopy over his head, so he is not getting wet. But he worries that because of the rain, he may lose his audience.

"If you promise to stay, I'll leave the canopy and stand out in the rain too," he offers.

Most of the people raise their hands, voting to stay. He moves to the edge of the canopy and preaches with the rain beating down on his head. And thousands of people listen—some with umbrellas, some without. Unfortunately, the rain that night was just the first. It rains on average every second night. Three or four nights each week, he steps out from the canopy and preaches in the chilling rain.

Seven thousand Bibles are given to people attending the meetings. That's one Bible for every 20 homes in the city. The program is making a large impact in this small city. For most of these people it is the first time they have ever seen or held a copy of the Scriptures. A bodyguard employed by the team is one of those who receive a free Bible. He spends most of his spare time reading it.

In the past, no Carter team has ever had more than one or two people fall sick. But here an illness that causes high fever and diarrhoea has broken out. Two American doctors on the team are working overtime to care for team members. Some nights Carter is walking on the stage with a raging fever. Preaching while soaking wet doesn't help his health.

As the days go by, the attendance slowly slides to about 4000 or 5000. And as it does, the demeanour of the people changes. They are no longer drinking, smoking and talking during the meetings. They are rapidly becoming a reverent, worshipping congregation.

Considering the aggravation of the rain, it is astonishing that the crowds keep coming back. It shows that Carter is delivering something the people really want. Nonetheless, there has been a huge drop-off in attendance. The percentage attending in the third week is the lowest percentage he has seen in a series in Russia. He feels the open-air venue is the cause.

One member of the Carter team sees someone staggering weakly into the stadium.

"Are you sick?" the team member asks.

"No," the weak man replies. "I've not eaten for three days. I've been saving my money for train fares to come to the meetings."

The man is an unemployed Siberian schoolteacher who taught English. He has a six-hour train journey to get to the meetings each night, and another six hours to get home. The first night he came just to hear someone speaking in English. But after that first meeting, he feels he has to keep coming. Hearing of his plight, the Carter team provide money for the teacher to pay for his train fares and to buy food.

Another person who frequently attends is a bishop from a church called "The Old Believers." The Old Believers and the Orthodox

Church separated centuries ago. Ever since, Old Believers have been a persecuted minority. The bishop is impressed by what he hears at Carter's program here in Irkutsk.

One evening he comes to see Carter after the meeting. "You are a gift of God sent to help us," he asserts. "Our city needs to hear this gospel message you are bringing us. You are most welcome here. I thank you on behalf of my people."

The two talk together, eat together, pray together and hug each other like Russian bears. A photo of their meeting becomes a front-page photograph on the worldwide edition of *Adventist Review*.

Then without warning and even though Carter has a legally binding contract, the manager of the sports stadium orders him out. He wants to use the stadium for a football match. By this stage the nightly audience is small enough to fit into the city's largest covered hall, but only if they hold two sessions. But being expelled from the sports stadium gives them one significant advantage. For the last week of their meetings, it doesn't matter if it rains.

Changing to the indoor venue seems like a simple decision, but it sends the technical staff into a frenzy. Normally it takes several days to set up the sound systems and electronics for a Carter program. Today they have to do it in eight hours. They unplug the whole system from the old venue and rewire everything in the new venue. He has set them an impossible deadline. The technicians are still plugging in vital cables as the audience walks in. But they achieve the impossible. When Carter walks onto the stage, it all works—and the audience doesn't know how close they are to not having a meeting.

The 26-day program ends with the coldest water at a baptism Carter has ever experienced. Despite this, 762 people commit their lives to God, including two university professors and many university students. The small Adventist community in the city will now have more than 1000 people attending.

Two full-time Russian pastors are allocated the task of caring for both the new converts and those yet to make decisions. They hire a beautiful trade union centre for the new church's weekly services. *The Carter Report* will pay the rent for this hall for the next 12 months. Plus the existing church will keep operating in another building. The members of the existing church divide themselves between the two churches so both congregations will include established members.

The Carter Report presents gifts to the new local church. They receive a $US3000 public-address system, an electronic keyboard and thousands of Bibles for follow-up meetings.

It is impossible to know if more people would have been baptised if the weather had been better. But it is wonderful to have so many new beacons for truth in this isolated corner of the world.

BROKEN GLASS DOORS

The Soviet Union was always at the forefront of space science and discovery. It was the first nation to launch a satellite into space. And it was the first nation to put a man in space. Even 10 years after the fall of the USSR, work in space is still important to the people.

The city of Dnepropetrovsk (pronounced *Nepro-petrovx*) is significant in the space program. Rockets for launching satellites are built here in conjunction with the American Boeing aircraft company.

Dnepropetrovsk—"space city"—is a seven-hour bus ride from Kiev, the capital of Ukraine. It's located on the banks of the Dnieper River, from which it derives its name. Much of the nation's space industry to build its giant space rockets and their minuscule components is here. However, the locals pay a high price for this. Largely because of the industrial pollution, their life expectancy is 30 years less than for a Westerner. Carter himself is badly affected by the pollution here. For one of the few periods in his life, he cancels his daily brisk walk because of the poor air quality.

The city produced what was called the "Dnepropetrovsk clan," a small group of locals who had a huge influence on running the entire USSR. The "clan" was founded by Leonid Brezhnev, who became General Secretary of the Communist Party and President of the Supreme Soviet. His "clan" controlled top levels of the Communist Party and the USSR for 20 years.

Like most Ukrainian cities, Dnepropetrovsk has a large sports stadium. The Communist government put a lot of money into sporting facilities as a deliberate substitute for religion. Now Carter has booked the city's Palace of Sport to build up the religion the "palace" was designed to replace.

It is never easy to organise meetings like this. More than a dozen government departments must give their permission for such meetings. No matter how tenuous one department's link is to the project, their signature is still vital. Gathering signatures has become an art form for the Carter team, to be done carefully and tactfully. The first signature is the Governor's. The last one is the fire warden's. They—or anyone in between—can stop the project. And any one of them may feel a need for a bribe before they give approval. The corruption of the Communist era continues 10 years after Communism has fallen.

The miracle of getting all these signatures is only the beginning. A similar miracle is needed to hire public halls to serve as churches for the new converts. If a Carter program baptises about 1300 people—as it will in Dnepropetrovsk—they will need as many as seven public halls afterwards. And these halls need to be secured in advance because the Carter team can't wait until the day after the baptisms before they start to find the necessary accommodation. Booking the halls requires another round of signing contracts and collecting signatures from officialdom. In all, as many as 100 signatures are required to book the halls for the Carter meetings and the follow-up church services.

It is 2001, 10 years since Carter preached his first evangelistic meetings in the USSR. The grand opening of Carter's latest evangelistic program is tomorrow. The team has done this many times. They operate like a well-oiled machine.

Inside the Palace of Sport, they set up their equipment for rehearsals. There are five powerful projectors to beam images onto large screens beside and behind the stage. These projectors operate through a giant transformer. This piece of equipment also "cleans" the power supply and prevents power surges. Because it weighs almost 100 kilograms (200 pounds), it is awkward to manoeuvre. In position, the power starts up but almost immediately it closes down. Whenever they turn on the switch, they get power for about one second, then nothing. They have no power—so there can be no rehearsal and there may be no meeting.

It is 5 pm on Friday when the transformer fails. The program starts in less than 24 hours. It is far too late to fly in a replacement for the faulty transformer.

A team member calls the equipment's manufacturer in New York. "We've never heard of this problem happening before," the technical support officer says. "It's probably been damaged in transit. There's nothing we can do to help you."

Abandoned by the only people who know what they are doing, the Carter team has to repair the transformer themselves. Carter suggests some of them pray. They gather in a huddle. "The program in this city is not our work, dear Lord, it is Yours. Please make this transformer work."

One of the Carter volunteers is Bob Ludwig, who was a sound engineer for the singer Michael Jackson. After prayer, he sees the problem in a new light. He will try to reverse the polarity. He removes that wire and connects this one. Ludwig later says he felt so foolish that he didn't pray when the problem first arose.

Carter can do nothing so he decides to leave. As he is getting into the car, someone runs out of the Palace of Sport, shouting, "Its working! It's working!" In response, he whispers softly, "Thank You, God. Thank You."

The following afternoon the program begins on time as if nothing had gone wrong.

American evangelist James Gilley came here in 1992 and strengthened the Protestant outpost in this city of 1.1 million people. Carter has come to build on his foundation. But nine years after Communism fell, the people in the city have developed a new security. Will they be attracted to the Carter program?

Carter has an unofficial way to judge the success of his opening program's advertising: how many glass doors are broken at the front of a city's Palace of Sport. When the surging crowds have pushed against the doors in other cities, the doors have shattered from the pressure. Here there are five broken doors leaving shattered glass across the front of the stadium. Clearly, Dnepropetrovsk is just as interested in prophecy and archaeology as Gorky, Kiev or St Petersburg.

There are four identical opening sessions, two on Saturday and two on Sunday. The Palace of Sport seats 6000, but far more than that fill each session. One of the opening sessions has 9000 people crammed inside. It is astonishing to see so many people standing so quietly for the 60-minute meeting. In total, the opening attendance is 30,000, the largest crowd to attend a public meeting in the city's 250-year history.

Overcrowding continues into the second, third and fourth nights. People are literally fighting each other to get the seats they want. Hopefully, the gospel will change that attitude.

Carter looks out across this vast auditorium. In the audience he sees a group of 60 Ukrainian soldiers with their commanding officer. He sees a man with no legs sitting on a flat platform with small wheels. He obviously doesn't have the money to buy a genuine wheelchair. On his left, he sees a large group of deaf people. Someone is using sign language to pass on Carter's message to them.

Most in the audience are atheists. But at the end of the first meeting, he asks them to stand for prayer. There is a rumble right across the auditorium. When people stand for prayer, their seats fold up making a dull thud. Six thousand dull thuds make one impressive rumble. And almost all these atheists are now impressed enough by Christianity to stand for prayer. For most, this is the first time they have prayed in their lives.

Carter plans to run two meetings each weeknight, at 5 pm and 7 pm. Then as the audience numbers dwindle, he plans to amalgamate the two meetings. But the numbers do not grow smaller as he expected. At the end of the second week 8000 people are still attending each night. They still need two sessions.

The staff doing hundreds of jobs behind the scenes have walkie-talkies to communicate with each other. A voice crackles out, "There's a man backstage prowling around with a pistol in his hand." Javier Piraino, a volunteer from California, is high above checking the floodlights. He calls back through the walkie-talkie, "Tell John's bodyguard to get him." And the man translating walkie-talkie messages then repeats this instruction in the Ukrainian language.

Carter and the translator are on the stage preaching with enthusiasm. They have absolutely no idea of the danger just the thickness of a curtain behind them.

His bodyguard quietly slips into the backstage area. He sees the man with the pistol. Then he puts himself in a position to disarm him. Other staff members rush in once the bodyguard has the gun. It is obvious the man is drunk. They check his pistol. He's forgotten to load it! This man was too drunk to remember the bullets.

Carter preaches about Christ's second coming on the first night of the second week. Because he is in "space city," he uses illustrations from the space program. He guides the audience to open their Bibles to 1 Thessalonians 4:16, 17 where Paul wrote about the Second Coming, "The dead in Christ will rise first," he reads in English. Then the translator echoes it in Ukrainian. "Then we who are left alive will be taken up with them in the clouds to meet the Lord in the air."

Carter tells his Dnepropetrovsk audience that at the Second Coming, they can all "meet the Lord in the air." It will not just be the cosmonauts who leave the earth. Each person in this audience can personally travel through space. "Reserve your seats now," he tells them. "This will be a space flight that has no chance of failure."

Although the Carter team has booked the Palace of Sport every night for four weeks, the Ukrainian president wants it for summit meetings with the presidents of two neighbouring nations. To entertain them, he wants to hold a boxing tournament. Carter's watertight contract to hire the hall means nothing. The president's need means they will have to miss one night of meetings. The boxing match is heavily promoted on television and draws an attendance of 3000. It gives the team a lot of satisfaction, knowing their advertising attracted 30,000.

The team are concerned that missing one program may break the habit of people attending each night. But the night after the boxing tournament, the attendance and the program continue as normal.

One woman coming to Carter's meetings is dying. Her doctor has told her she has incurable cancer. Larissa and her family have attended the meetings for several weeks. As they listen, their trust in God grows. Their hope of eternal life increases. And as it does, they see that God doesn't just grant life for eternity; He also grants it here and now.

Near the end of the series of meetings, Larissa and her family meet with Carter privately and tell him about the cancer. He suggests they return the following evening and come backstage between the 5 pm and 7 pm meetings.

The following night Carter and several Ukrainian pastors open their Bibles to James 5:14. They read it aloud to Larissa and her family. "Are any of you ill? They should call for the elders of the church and have them pray over them and anoint them with olive oil in the Lord's name. This request offered in faith will heal the sick. The Lord will raise them. And if they have committed any sins, they will be forgiven."

The small group gathered here solemnly follows this guideline. Carter and the other pastors pray that God will heal Larissa. Carter dips his finger in a small jar of olive oil. Then he gently rubs his finger with the oil in a small circle on her forehead.

A few days later, there is a baptism. Among the 1281 people baptised are some of the deaf people, the man without legs, and some of the soldiers. And Larissa and her brother are also baptised.

Carter returns to America. Each summer he tries to hold a month-long evangelistic series in a former USSR city. Then each winter he returns to the former USSR and holds one-day meetings in each of the cities where he has previously preached. These meetings strengthen the new church members. And they also encourage some people back to church who have left their commitment.

So six months after his major series here, Carter has now returned to Dnepropetrovsk. Among those who greet him is Larissa. She is still alive. With joy written all over her face, she tells him what happened to her. He asks her recount her story to the combined meeting of the city's nine Christian Adventist churches.

Larissa walks onto the stage in front of 2000 people. It's something she had never done before. But her nervousness quickly fades as she tells that she had incurable cancer. With little time left to live, she came to the meetings at the Palace of Sport. There she asked God to come into her life. He did. And her life became wonderful.

Larissa then turns to face Carter, who is standing on the stage beside her. Tears run down her cheeks. She thanks him for showing her the way of salvation. And the whole audience calls out, "Amen."

Then Larissa tells the audience how the pastors had seen her a few days before her baptism. They had rubbed her forehead with olive oil, as the Bible said to do. After her baptism, Larissa says she returned to her doctor and he thoroughly examined her. He couldn't find any trace of cancer in her body. The cancer was completely gone. The doctor pronounced her healed.

The whole audience is delighted and calls out, *"Slava Bogu! Slava Bogu! Slava Bogu!"*—"Praise God! Praise God! Praise God!"

Carter's Manager Arrested for Murder

The Carter team doesn't have enough cash for the campaign in Kharkov. John Carter has urgently dictated a two-page newsletter to supporters in America. He tells of the success of the opening weekend. Then he says frankly, "No funds remain." Carter's office in California urgently mails the newsletter. Funds quickly come in so the program can continue.

Carter's office transfers the money to a local bank in Kharkov (pronounced *Har-coff*). Team manager Alexander Antonyuk goes to the bank to pick up the money. It is only a simple task but things go horribly wrong.

As Alexander's minibus stops at the team's hotel, he's grabbed by four armed men. He is carrying $60,000 in US currency, and they want the money. While they are not in uniform, the men claim to be police. They arrest him for murder.

The men say that they are working on a series of brutal murders. There's been a lot of media publicity about these deaths. And when there is such publicity, police become more anxious to get an arrest. Possibly the police have recognised Alexander's minibus numberplate as being from out of town and are suspicious. When they arrest him, they claim he is the hit man for the murders. And they claim the money was his payment for the crimes.

The other theory is that crooked police were tipped off by a bank teller about the large withdrawal of cash. (Bank tellers who tip off the Mafia or dishonest police about large withdrawals receive a percentage of the money.) Or it's possible that the police found out about the cash by tapping the Carter team's telephones. The money is a significant temptation because $60,000 is what a police officer in Russia would have earned in a lifetime. If the police are crooked, it's almost certain Alexander will never be seen live again.

Fortunately, as the police grab Alexander, Pastor Harold Harker (the Australian representative of *The Carter Report*) is at the front of the hotel. Alexander calls to him for help. Harker gets in the front seat of the mini-van so the police can't take Alexander away without taking him too.

Harker calls for Carter. About a minute later Carter comes out of the hotel front door and sees what's happening. "I immediately threw myself into the battle," Carter says afterwards. "I put my arms around Alexander and said [in English] 'This is my man. He works for me.'"

The police recognise Carter's face. And while they don't understand English, they know from his body language what he means.

When other church members come out of the hotel, Carter shouts, "Run for Vadim and tell him to come out. Run for David and tell him to bring the TV camera."

When Vadim arrives, Carter explains through the translator why Alexander has the money and what he is doing with it. He says the money does not belong to Alexander; he was just collecting it from the bank.

"Well, you've lost your money," says the police officer, who clearly doesn't want to give back the cash.

"It's our money," Carter argues. "It was wired to us from America. You can check with the bank."

But the police don't seem interested in checking.

A crowd of Carter team members has formed in front of the hotel. They stand there as witnesses, putting pressure on the police by their presence.

David Carter is applying even more pressure. He has a professional TV camera and is recording everything that happens. If Alexander disappears, David will have video evidence of the last police to have seen him alive.

"We are recording what you are doing today for American TV," John Carter tells the police.

The police keep insisting they have to take Alexander and the money. Carter's team keeps insisting that they must not.

The police push Alexander into the minibus, preparing to drive it away. Carter joins Harker in the bus's front seats so the police can't drive it. The stand-off lasts 90 minutes.

It is a battle of the wills. Whoever has the strongest will gets Alexander—and the money.

About 30 minutes into the stand-off, Carter tells Harker to get a *Carter Report* advertising brochure from the hotel. It has a photo of Carter on it. He hopes this will help persuade the police they are genuine.

Carter is treating this as an innocent mistake by the police. He explains to the police that the money was to help pay for his meetings, and the photo and brochure is evidence he is running an expensive program. But the police do not accept his argument.

Some team members are praying. Others are too stunned to know what to do.

The police ask Carter, "Who owns this money? Do you own it?"

"No! The Lord in heaven owns it!" Carter replies.

The police laugh. They think Carter's comment is funny. It's brought some humour into a very serious situation.

Eventually, the police give in and Carter shakes hands with each of the police officers. He thanks them for the work they are doing against the drug trade. As they drive away, Harker gets out of the mini-van and David Carter turns off his video camera. The Carter team takes the money to a safe place.

Key members of the team meet the next day in Carter's hotel room. They decide that Alexander should see the chief of police personally and arrange an appointment for the next day.

"You're in the clear," the police chief tells Alexander. "It was just a case of mistaken identity."

THE KGB COLONEL AND THE POLITICIAN

Among those mingling in the crowd at the Carter program is a senior officer of the KGB. He had slowly risen through the ranks and became a colonel. He was a KGB Professor of Atheism, teaching young Russian soldiers about the evils of religion. His job was to brainwash them into accepting that there is no God.

Also in the crowd is a senior politician, a member of the Ukraine parliament. He has risen through the ranks of those wanting power, and wanting to serve the nation. He has high status in society and he is the brother of the nation's president.

The two take their seats in separate places and automatically look around, mentally checking the venue. The Kharkov Palace of Sport is reconfigured with seats on the floor to increase its capacity to about 5000. A large temporary stage is generously decorated with flowers and has a professional-quality electronic keyboard. Dominating the stage is a blackboard 12 metres (40 feet) long, with about 20 "black light" fluorescent tubes to make chalk glow when the speaker writes on the board. At the rear of the stage are two large screens. A metal tower stands in the audience, supporting projectors, lights and PA system speakers. A woman is sitting at the top of the tower at a control panel. The whole thing looks impressive.

But the colonel and the politician have not come to the meeting as spies. If you asked them why they are here, they would probably say they have come because of the advertising—or perhaps they are here to see how feeble Christianity really is. But these long-time opponents of religion are probably here because God's Spirit has drawn them.

Because of their experience, the two feel they are experts on religion. But a Westerner and a local walk on the stage—one speaking in English, the other translating—and in just a few minutes the two realise the religion at this meeting is nothing like anything they have encountered previously.

In each meeting Carter upholds the Bible as the Word of God. At all the programs of the first week, the colonel and the politician listen as Carter argues that the Bible can be trusted. This is all done with nonstop photographs projected onto the giant screens. The two men cannot find flaws in Carter's arguments that prove there is a God.

At the beginning of the second week, the format of the program changes dramatically. The colonel, the politician and everyone else in the audience are each given a Bible. The stadium is kept bright so the audience can open their Bibles and read the verses Carter is quoting.

Carter doesn't place Bible verses on the screen because that doesn't make a physical connection to the Book itself. He has a Bible and opens it whenever he has a verse to read. He tells the audience the page numbers. And because everyone is using the same edition of the Bible, the audience easily finds each verse. Having the audience turn up each verse makes the audience an eyewitness of what the Bible says. His plan is that the audience can see what Scripture says for themselves. So the colonel and the politician get firsthand knowledge of what the Bible says.

Carter's lectures for the next three weeks are based on the same passage of Scripture, Revelation 14:6-12. The first theme is "the everlasting gospel" (verse 6). The colonel and the politician read that God's salvation is a "free gift" (see Romans 6:23). Their hearts are strangely warmed.

The next night he talks about the man who wrote his own life story before he was born. The two open their Bibles to read astonishing prophecies that pinpoint Jesus as the Messiah.

The next three nights are what Carter calls "blockbusters." They are all on the antichrist, a theme John also draws from Revelation 14.

On the third Monday night, neither the colonel nor the politician comes to the meeting. It is for young people only. The local conference youth leaders run a mainly musical program for youth. Two nights in the series are like this. They are designed to bond together the existing church young people and those about to join the church. Carter wants them to become a group. He wants them all to have a sense of belonging.

The colonel and the politician attend six other meetings this week. Carter tells the audience these meetings are another six "blockbusters." The six programs explore the state of the dead (in two sessions), the occult, the Sabbath, health and tithing.

The fourth and final week of the meetings are all programs about making a decision. In the meetings, Carter explains what the Bible says about baptism. Some here in Kharkov accept it; some reject it.

What will the colonel and the politician do? They have both spent a lifetime as leaders of Christianity's opposition. Surely, their status is much too high to become involved with a mere Protestant church. But one of them takes a pen. He writes the name *Vladimir Ivanenko* on the card requesting Christian baptism.

Vladimir wakes up on the morning of what he has always regarded as a secular day. But now he accepts it as the Sabbath. And on this particular Sabbath, June 6, 2002, he will be baptised. He is one of 1121 baptised at Kharkov.

But there should have been one more. The politician is not baptised. He doesn't want to risk his status and position.

In contrast, the KGB colonel is overwhelmed with gratitude. Because of the power and position he has, the colonel could afford to buy a substantial gift of thanks. Instead, he chooses something humble, in line with his lowly position as a newborn Christian.

A few days earlier he took a small amount of silver into the workshop at his home and began to fashion it into a new shape. This will be a gift to Carter. He will present it to him personally and privately.

It is now the last Saturday night of Carter's meetings in Kharkov. After Carter says the final prayer, the colonel makes his way to the back of the stage and says, "I was baptised today."

He gives Carter the gift he has fashioned with his own hands, a silver cross. "I give this to you because in these meetings I have learned to love the Christ who died on the cross. Take this as a sign of the power of God to change the heart of an old atheist."

It is a poignant moment, one Carter believes he will never forget. He later writes about that moment on his website. "Could you imagine it? Here is a man from the world's most sinister organisation giving me a symbol of Christ dying for the sins of the whole world. How great are the love and the grace of God! How wonderful is His power to save to the uttermost all those who come to God through the Lord Jesus. Just think: If God can do this for a tough old KGB officer, He can do it for anyone. No-one is hopeless."

May 2003

GOD VERSUS THE MAFIA

The Mafia almost runs the city of Odessa. It's a popular holiday destination for people in the former USSR. Organised crime in this city is so organised they have their own permanent office. It's in the Palace of Sport.

The Mafia is prominent in sponsoring sport in Ukraine. They are especially generous with their sponsorship of judo, boxing and wrestling. When someone wins a tournament in those sports, the Mafia will give them a Mercedes-Benz. In this way they lure the strong men of judo, boxing and wrestling into their organisation and the Mafia's "enforcers" are among the toughest men in the city.

Carter is scheduled to hold an evangelistic series in Odessa and he has booked the Palace of Sport for his meetings. The Mafia leaders were on a trip to Spain when brochures advertising *The Carter Report* were distributed, so the program started without their "permission." Returning to the city, they are angry about what is happening.

Normally "the Mob" would do their intimidation and blackmail in secret. But they have so much power in Odessa they plan to threaten this preacher from the West in a public way. They decide to "get"

Carter on the stage while his meeting is in progress.

Carter and his translator walk onto the stage, not knowing their plan to burst onto the platform part way through the meeting. The Carter team has paid for a police presence at all the meetings but tonight they notice the police are not here. Carter starts speaking on the subject of "The strange world of the occult" and his translator closely echoes his words. Some 5500 people are listening to everything they say. "The Mob" plans that those 5500 will witness Mafia intimidation and Mafia authority.

The Mafia "enforcers" know this building well, so it's not hard for them to make their way backstage. They are about to pounce.

Carter and the translator are startled by a noise behind them, but Carter keeps preaching and the translator follows. Both of them know something is wrong but they don't know what it is. At the back of the stage they can hear a noise like people fighting. However, the two keep going as if nothing is wrong. The noise of a fight continues a little longer, and then it stops. When the meeting ends, Carter and his translator are told that the Mafia planned to publicly humiliate them in a face-to-face encounter on stage.

But Carter had taken precautions.

Because the former USSR has become such a dangerous place, *The Carter Report* team includes a bodyguard. He is a former soldier, who knows how to take care of himself and how to care for Carter. He is standing at the backstage door at the moment the Mafia try to burst in. He is outnumbered, but because he is defending a narrow entrance, he gets the upper hand against larger numbers. The Mafia members retreat—at least for now.

The next morning, the Odessa city officials find out what has happened and step in. Carter's meetings have become too popular with the masses to have them prematurely stopped. The city officials hold an urgent meeting with the Mafia leaders, and the Mafia agrees to pull back and let *The Carter Report* continue.

An estimated 15 per cent of the population of Odessa has HIV/AIDS. Some are innocent victims, such as those who have contracted the infection through blood transfusions or who are born with it. But most have it from illicit sexual contact. It has given Odessa the highest rate of HIV/AIDS infection in the industrialised world.

Still, this city of a million people is a magnet, with 50 kilometres (30 miles) of beaches attracting tourists from Eastern Europe and as far away as North America. Single American males come here to find a Ukrainian girl and take her home as a bride. But they can also take home AIDS.

Carter is holding two identical sessions of his meetings each night in Odessa. Most sessions are full and usually several hundred people are turned away because there aren't enough seats. That means he is speaking to 11,000 people daily and on average about 1600 have the HIV virus. Knowing this sad reality, he has a special sense of urgency in his preaching here.

Carter had not wanted to preach in Odessa. Plans were well advanced for him to preach in another major city but that city's mayor died late in the negotiation stage. The Carter team could have waited for another mayor to be elected, but the new mayor may not have been cooperative. So instead of taking the risk of not holding any meetings at that time, church leaders suggest Carter preaches in Odessa.

But it is the wrong time of year. The city is crammed with people on holidays. And the locals are working frenetically to meet the needs of holiday-makers. But at the end of the four-week program,

Carter concludes that holding the meetings at this "wrong" time of the year was part of God's plan.

One reason for this was because of Ivor and his wife. They had travelled 5000 kilometres (3000 miles) from Siberia to holiday in Odessa. A brochure for *The Carter Report* was delivered to their holiday apartment. The meetings seemed to be something different. With time on their hands, they join the crush at the front doors of the Palace of Sport. Fortunately, they are among the people able to get inside the opening meeting. Police turn many people away for crowd-control reasons.

Night by night, the Bible comes alive for the Siberian couple. At one meeting, Carter asks the audience to raise their hands if they want to follow God's plan for their lives. The Siberian couple raise their hands. Another night they stand when he asks who will pledge to keep God's Sabbath. After three weeks they almost run to the front of the auditorium when he asks people to come forward if they want to be baptised. A long way from home, they are baptised with about 650 others in the warm waters of the Black Sea.

Beverley Carter still remembers seeing the Siberian couple's faces when they came out of the water. They were beaming with delight.

Because *The Carter Report* was held at the "wrong" time of the year, this Siberian couple heard the gospel and gave their hearts to God. But their conversion has a special significance. They live in a city in Siberia that has no Protestant churches. Several times the Adventist Church had tried to hold public meetings in that city, but were prevented. Despite the end of Communism, Protestant missionaries in this city still risk death.

But while the church couldn't take the gospel to that Siberian city, the people from that city could hear the gospel elsewhere. What a holiday the Siberian couple had! They return home from Odessa on fire. Their plan is to start a church in their home city. And because they actually live in the city, the political powers will find it difficult to stop them.

And other stories can be told of people who committed their lives to Christ in Odessa:

Maria is the daughter of a Jewish rabbi. Her parents were murdered by the Nazis. More recently, she lost both of her sons at the hands of terrorists. "I came to John Carter's meetings looking for a real hope that lasts beyond death. I'm very grateful for the Living Word being preached here and for the hope I am finding. I am bringing my fellow Jews to the meetings so they too can find the true Messiah." A few days after she wrote those words on a response card, Maria was baptised in the Black Sea.

Olga travelled from the adjoining nation of Moldova to come to the Odessa meetings. She hated the state church in her country because it had persecuted her family but she didn't necessarily hate God. Fourteen years earlier she developed breast cancer and was given two years to live. She prayed to "the God I do not know." In a dream she was told that she would not die, but would live. She survived her breast cancer. God obviously had an important reason for her to live on, and she found that reason when she heard the gospel preached in Odessa. "I have now begun a new life," she says. "I feel better and I sleep better. I have discovered a new purpose in my life. I have found salvation."

Anna was raised in a home with a strong emphasis on atheism. For 17 years her mother was secretary of the local branch of the Communist Party. If Anna wanted to read a book, her parents made her read the Communist classics. She was specifically forbidden to read the Bible. Thanks to the Carter program, she now has a Bible of her own. She is astonished by what she has found in it. She's attended all 26 meetings in Odessa and was baptised in the Black Sea. "I have found salvation," she says.

Alexander is 70 years old, very old by local standards. When he received a handbill about the meetings, he thought of his mother who had prayed for him as a boy in a remote Siberian village. He is now following his mother's Saviour and believes the Carter meetings are the answer to prayers his mother prayed half-a-century earlier.

Valentina travelled 80 kilometres (50 miles) by bus each day to attend the Odessa meetings. As a little girl she was forced to watch Communist police officers gang-rape her mother. Her mother was killed in 1944 and Valentina was raised in an orphanage. After a life of horrors, she has now found hope and peace in Christ.

Tatiana decided to commit suicide. She went to the market to buy food for a week. Then she planned to cook it for her husband before killing herself. Coming home from the market, she saw an angel. This changed everything. She came to Carter's meetings and this changed things even more. At the meetings she made a series of decisions, committing herself to Christ. "After I was baptised, I found the reason to live," she says.

Irina is a university student. She was impressed by the meeting's evidence from archaeology and prophecy. "I have decided to give my life for the glory of God," she says. "But I want religion that is not just form and ceremony. I need an experience that changes my life, and provides the answers to my questions. And that is what I have found."

A BRIEF HISTORY OF THE USSR

One hundred years ago, Russia was ruled by the Tsar. Alternatively translated *Czar*, that's a Russian version of the name Caesar. So the Russian royalty were effectively claiming the same title as the rulers of ancient Rome.

The Tsar engaged in an enormous engineering project, building the Trans-Siberian Railway. This single project took most of the money that should have gone into running the country. As a result, almost everything else the Government was supposed to do in Russia wasn't getting done. This created dissatisfaction with the government. It also created a climate where rebellion was possible. And in fact, a rebellion eventually happened in 1917, which brought the Communists to power.

Communism is a political theory developed by the German-born philosopher Karl Marx. He argued that everyone is equal and to be happy people don't have to have private property. So the Communist government confiscated most private property in the nation. However, this didn't make people happy.

And while everyone was supposed to be equal, it didn't work out that way either. Some people had more equality than others. The Communist bosses lived with the same sort of extravagant wealth as the Tsars they replaced. But most other people were poor.

There is another thing one should know about the Communists. They said there was no God. And they persecuted people who said there was.

Russia was the scene of the most brutal fighting in World War II. At the end of that war, Russia (actually the USSR) took effective control of many countries in Eastern Europe. British Prime Minister Winston Churchill, in a speech at an American university, declared that an iron curtain had descended across Europe. The term "iron curtain" was quickly adopted in the West. The Communist areas then became known as the Iron Curtain countries.

The USSR at this time was controlled by a dictator named Joseph Stalin. To keep control of his country and make it run the way he wanted, he killed an estimated 50 million of his own people.

After World War II, the United States and the USSR both increased their weapons of war. These became the two most powerful military machines the world had ever seen. For the first time in history, the armed forces had the ability to destroy the entire planet in just a few minutes. It was called the Cold War, but it had the weapons to become extremely hot.

Under Communism, the government owned all the factories and farms in the USSR. That meant it could sell everything at low prices to keep the people happy. The trouble with selling everything at a loss is that money needs to come from somewhere. But the government had a solution for that too. They owned all the oilwells. And they sold their oil to Europe at huge profits. So oil kept all the economic wheels turning properly.

In the early 1980s, US President Ronald Reagan called the USSR "the evil empire." He then created a secret plan to destroy that empire.

The plan was simple and devastating. The USA used its economic might to win all the oil contracts in Europe. This had the side effect of creating low oil prices for a decade. But its main result was that the USSR government ran out of money.

There was a second secret part of Ronald Reagan's plan, although in one way it wasn't all that secret. He publicly announced that the United States was going to use new technology to make satellites that could destroy intercontinental missiles. This became known as the Star Wars project.

The USSR took the bait and decided to do the same thing. It was incredibly expensive—just like building the Trans-Siberian Railway. And the result was the same. Other government projects didn't get the money they needed. There was huge discontent. And there wasn't much else. There were shortages of everything. It was common to stand in a line for six hours just to buy a loaf of bread.

The third part of President Reagan's plan was carried out jointly with the Pope, who happened to be from an Iron Curtain country. The plan was to exploit every piece of discontent that occurred in the USSR and its eastern European allies. And the Pope had the status and the influence to exploit a lot of discontent.

At this time, the USSR had a new president, Mikhail Gorbachev. He saw that people in Western countries had more incentive that those in the USSR. He believed openness and freedom would also give his people more incentive. However, it also gave his people more freedom to complain about the terrible financial situation.

In 1990, the USSR leaders passed laws giving their people religious freedom. But people in far-flung parts of the empire wanted a different type of freedom—freedom from control by Moscow. The USSR's leaders believed civil war was possible. To avoid that, they voted to divide the USSR into 15 separate republics.

In August 1991, the Russian people and the world became aware that the USSR was coming to an end. On December 1, 1991, it officially happened. The USSR ceased to exist and 15 independent republics took its place. The two best known of these republics are Ukraine and Russia. In fact, in area, Russia is still the largest country in the world.

When religious freedom came to the USSR, evangelists from many Western countries went there. The two most successful were both Seventh-day Adventists, Mark Finley and John Carter. The rollcall of evangelists who went to help the Russian people includes some of the biggest names from all denominations. But not even the great Billy Graham matched what these two Adventist evangelists achieved in what is now the former USSR.

John and Beverley Carter with their son, David, in the Australian country town of Parkes, New South Wales. Here, in 1965, the couple had their first baby and held their first evangelistic campaign.

John's mother, Jean Carter, photographed just before her death at age 91, in 2005.

Carter on location at the Great Pyramid in Egypt, filming his highly successful TV advertisements.

Carter (left) and Graeme Bradford (centre right) baptising death-row jail inmates in the Philippines. Several weeks after this photo was taken, all these new church members were executed in the electric chair.

A typical advertising brochure for a Carter program, this one for Manila in the Philippines in 1985.

Carter's program in Harare, Zimbabwe, in 1981 attracted the largest attendance ever to an Adventist evangelistic series in Africa.

On a Friday night in January 1991, Russian church members prayed that they would not die during the severe winter. The next morning instead of putting money in the offering plate at church, Carter told them to take an envelope of cash—as a gift from Carter's church in California—so they could buy food.

Carter's first baptism in Russia. New believers stood in 30 lines, with about 60 people in each line, waiting for their turn to be immersed in the Volga River.

David Carter filmed a later Nizhni baptism from a Russian helicopter.

Carter and KGB General Vladimir (centre) flanked by two KGB colonels. In a historic meeting in 1992, Carter explained Christianity to 1000 KGB trainees. He was the first Christian to preach to the KGB.

Carter with 3ABN television founder Danny Shelton at Carter's first major campaign in Russia. Shelton's TV network raised money to build a church for the new believers. The Christian Cultural Center is the largest Protestant building in Russia.

Four Russian soldiers baptised in Carter's campaign in Nizhni Novgorod. One of them disappeared, apparently murdered by the Mafia. The other three started an Adventist church in their city.

Sergei was one of three Mafia men who committed themselves to Christ at Carter's first major series in Russia. As a result, Mafia leaders sentenced them to death.

Dr Julia Outkina was baptised in Carter's first Russian evangelistic series. She is now known nationwide in Russia as host of the Christian TV program "Face to Face."

A church under construction at the Volga Auto Plant in Russia. The congregation was formed after a Carter campaign in the city. The church building was paid for by a Carter supporter from California.

The first Protestant church built in the Russian city of Dzerzinsk, considered the most polluted city in the world. Money for the church was donated by the Greek Adventist community in Melbourne, Australia. The church was established by an "accidental" Carter campaign.

Glass doors broken by the pressure of the crowds have been a frequent sight at Carter's evangelistic campaigns in the former USSR.

When Carter gave out Bibles to use in his meetings, people arrived several hours early to read the Bibles before the meeting started.

The result of powerful advertising! In 1995, government officials in Kiev had huge crowd-control problems. About 100,000 people arrived at a Carter campaign but the hall had only 9500 seats.

Russian audiences were astounded—and excited—when Carter gave them free Bibles. In his preaching, Carter gets the audience to open to every Bible verse he reads.

The crowd at Carter's Kiev meetings, which at its conclusion saw about 3500 people baptised in the Dnieper River.

In this auditorium in Kiev, Nikita Khrushchev announced, "Christianity will be banished from the earth." However, three decades later, Carter holds follow-up meetings for new Christians baptised six months earlier.

With 2400 seats, this Adventist church in Kiev is the largest Protestant church in Ukraine. It was partly financed by Carter's TV viewers to house some of the 3500 people a Carter campaign baptised in that city.

Beverley Carter (centre) provides for children in orphanages in every former USSR city where her husband preaches.

In 1995, John and Beverley Carter were responsible for the first United States Air Force flight to Ukraine after the Cold War. The Hercules aircraft was loaded with hospital equipment to help orphans and victims of Chernobyl.

Carter and translator Vadim Butov at the end of a meeting, at which 1000 atheists have come to the front to dedicate themselves to Christ.

Carter's son, David (left), and sound engineer Bob Ludwig directing TV coverage of Carter's St Petersburg evangelistic series.

President of the Southern California Conference, Bjarne Christensen, organising gifts for church members at the next stop along the Trans-Siberian Railway.

Carter with the locomotive of the Trans-Siberian Express on his pastoral rail journey in 1998.

This couple on holidays from Siberia was baptised with about 650 others in the Black Sea at Odessa. They were able to return to their home city and plant a church in a city where evangelism by Protestants was banned.

Crowds with umbrellas and rainwear in Carter's open-air evangelistic series in Siberia in 1999.

Carter's translator, Vadim Butov, with his wife, Helen, and baby, Paul. Helen is a medical doctor, but she regularly runs evangelistic series based on Carter's program.

"Paul the Prisoner" was imprisoned for years in a Communist "refrigerator cell" for printing Christian books. He has now printed Russian translations of two books written by Carter.

Vladimir Samorodkin was First Secretary of the Communist Party, a very senior position. He and his wife, Valentina, became Adventists by watching Carter's Russian TV program.

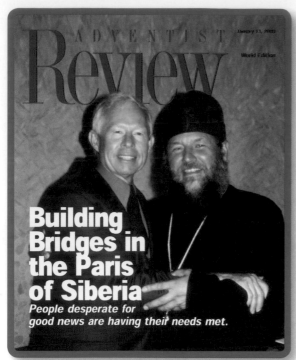

"Adventist Review" reports on John Carter's campaign in Irkutsk, Siberia. The Orthodox Bishop of the Old Believers exclaimed to John Carter, "You are a gift to us from heaven."

Carter's campaign manager, Alexander Antonyuk (left), with workers at a mushroom farm started by a man converted in a Carter campaign. In turn, the farm has become a simple way of winning people to Christ.

Carter baptising Billy Graham's organist Paul Michelson. Michelson said, "John Carter is Billy Graham's successor."

Susan Piraino, director of communications for The Carter Report, Inc, was baptised by John Carter during the Los Angeles campaign in 1990.

David Carter, John's son, is director of television production for The Carter Report.

John and Beverley Carter in Red Square, Moscow.

The Carter Report offices in Arcadia, California, USA. The site also includes a church and television production facility.

A NEWSPAPER HATE CAMPAIGN

Welcome to Zaporozhye. For the next two weeks the first task for John Carter each day will *not* be saying his morning prayer. Rather, he will check the flag on the government building outside his hotel window.

Carter has realised that this flag is a way of gauging air pollution. If the flag is pointing away from him, the air will be fairly pure and clean. If the flag is pointing toward him, pollution will be horrific.

The flag is pointing away today, so it will be a good day. Carter looks down from the window and has a clear view of the street below in both directions. It's called Lenin Street. The locals claim it is the longest street in Europe.

Carter raises his eyes to the skyline and he can see for about three kilometres (two miles), rather than the 500 metres it could be on a bad day. He can count 80 giant smokestacks from his window. Together they discharge about 300 tonnes of black and yellow smoke each day. These noxious fumes cause the million locals to have an extremely short life expectancy.

The daily pollution levels will be an important factor in Carter's program here. After a season of large Californian grassfires, he caught Valley Fever. It has damaged his lungs and dramatically reduced his endurance. He doesn't believe he can preach every night for a month. He plans to preach for only two weeks, and then have a colleague take the second two weeks of the program. However, if the pollution levels stay low, his lungs may give him more stamina. He may then be able to take the full four weeks of meetings.

Carter had planned to preach here 12 months earlier, but the city's mayor died during the negotiations. So his program was transferred to Odessa. But when the new mayor was elected, he requested Carter to come.

Advertising for *The Carter Report* is unlike anything the city has seen. The team has spent $US20,000 for half-a-million full-colour brochures. One brochure has been delivered to every home. They have spent $US30,000 for saturation TV advertising. They are running paid announcements on every local radio station. And they have posters in key outdoor locations across the city, plus posters on trams and buses.

However, the president of Ukraine wants to run an election rally in the stadium Carter has booked. He insists that the stadium manager cancel the contract with Carter. The stadium manager refuses. The president is furious. "When I am elected, I will finish you Adventists off," he warns.

The president speaks to people at the local radio and TV stations and buys advertising. In these ads he says the Carter meetings have been cancelled. The ads run the day after the program begins.

Carter and his team rush to each radio and TV station to buy advertising to say the meetings are still on. They can't risk losing their audience because of the false announcements. This extra advertising is expensive and they don't have money for it in their budget. But the money will come from somewhere.

The oldest church in Ukraine also opposes the Carter meetings. That church controls one of the city's daily newspapers. The newspaper sets an anti-Carter tone that will be followed by most of the other newspapers. Every day the papers run yet another article against the Carter meetings. Not once do these newspapers interview Carter or his team when writing their stories. Truth is not the important thing in their stories. The important thing is to turn people away from the program.

This is an isolated city and the locals are not used to foreigners and they are suspicious of outsiders. The newspapers play on that suspicion every day to give credibility to their constant attacks.

Their stories are anti-Protestant, anti-American, anti anything that's different. The articles say the Christian Adventists are a dangerous cult from America. Another article says the Adventists have come to destroy Ukraine's culture. Another says the Adventists are making war on the holy mother church. They also make personal attacks against Carter.

Fortunately, one daily newspaper has not joined this negative campaign. This newspaper sends one of its reporters to a Carter meeting. She writes a positive article. The reporter returns to the meetings in her own time. This woman has become so intrigued by what she has heard, she keeps coming. Carter expects she will be baptised.

The newspapers' hate campaign has reduced the numbers attending the meetings. But thousands of people are still coming. Carter notices this audience is different from others he has faced in the former USSR. They are more attentive. You can just "feel" the difference in this audience, he says. "I could hear a pin drop here in the Palace of Sport."

Back in his hotel room, Carter writes a report for his website. "I don't think that during a lifetime of preaching I have spoken to such an attentive, responsive audience. These dear people are like sponges soaking up the Water of life."

Perhaps the campaign by the newspapers is actually having a positive effect, removing people from the audience who are inclined to distract others. Or maybe the newspapers have made people think more deeply about why they are actually here.

Carter doesn't leave it to the last night of a series to encourage people to make decisions for God. Every time he preaches he asks the audience to make a decision. The first night here he asked the people to close their eyes, open their minds and pray. It may seem that this is a small decision, but it's actually a big step. Most of the people at each meeting on the first weekend have never prayed before. Many of them have never even heard of the concept of prayer, but Carter explains to them that prayer is like talking to God as a friend. Then most of them respond to his request to shut their eyes. It takes only a few more nights before almost everyone will close their eyes for prayer.

A few nights later, Carter's call for a decision requires more commitment. He asks those who want to accept Jesus as their Lord and Saviour to come forward. An amazing 1500 people walk to the front. He prays with them, asking God to confirm their decision.

By calling for regular decisions in his meetings, Carter is preparing the people for the big decision. He explains to a meeting of local pastors that a series of smaller decisions will produce better final results than calling for one big decision at the end.

The local team needs to know this because they will finish this series without Carter. The Valley Fever still leaves him weak. The pollution in the city further aggravates his lungs.

After two weeks John Carter passes the meetings over to *The Carter Report*'s program manager, Alexander Antonyuk, and flies home to California. After 15 years preaching behind the Iron Curtain, he bows out. Few people farewell him at the plane. No-one realises this may have been his last major evangelistic campaign in Russia or Ukraine.

Meanwhile, the opposition continues after Carter has gone. In fact, Alexander receives a death threat. He is told he will die if he keeps preaching. But he cannot give these people a taste of the gospel, and then desert them. Alexander ignores the threat and walks onto the stage.

The third Saturday night of a program is when Carter usually asks his audience to sign cards requesting baptism. Despite the continuing opposition, Alexander decides to follow this pattern. He explains the biblical importance of baptism and at the end of the meeting, he asks those who want to be baptised to come forward.

The following Saturday the team baptises 300 people. A week later a further 50 are baptised. It is the lowest figure Carter has ever had from a full series of meetings behind the former Iron Curtain. Yet those baptised during the Zaporozhye newspaper hate campaign seem to be a little more special than most.

ON THE CARTER TEAM

The *Carter Report* organisation operates from offices in Arcadia, California, USA. Its office is on busy Duarte Road, a four-lane street that carries 50,000 cars a day past the office. Most of the two acres is taken up by a car park for a church on the site. The office and TV studio are run by a small, close-knit staff of about a dozen people.

While John Carter was paid a salary as a church pastor, he also ran an organisation called *The Carter Report, Inc.* It has its own board of directors and is structured as a 501(c)(3) nonprofit tax-exempt company under United States law. As such, it must be entirely separate from the church. Carter makes sure its finances are "squeaky clean." The ministry operates to the highest ethical and accounting standards.

The Carter Report team members raise the money to run Carter's evangelistic programs. They prepare his TV and radio programs. And they do all the work to prepare and run the giant overseas evangelistic programs.

So let's meet a few of *The Carter Report*'s staff:

Donn Beagle is a professional sound engineer. He was working for a Hollywood sound studio when assigned to do audio work for Carter's meetings at Pasadena Civic Center. He had been praying to find a church. At the meeting, John Carter suggested Donn visit his church, which he did. "This felt like the church God wanted me to be in," Donn says.

In 1997 Donn was asked to do audio work for Carter's St Petersburg series. It was a big request because he would have to quit his job to go.

"I prayed about it and God said go. It was a test of my faith because for the whole month I was gone, I knew I had no job to come back to in America. And I had bills to pay."

When Donn returned home, he found a few short-term jobs. Then he told God, "You told me to quit my job and go to St Petersburg. I stepped out in faith. What are You going to do for me?" God's answer was to join *The Carter Report* team full time.

Donn now works in a large room filled with an amazing array of sound-recording equipment. What's even more amazing to an outsider is that he knows how to use all that equipment!

So what's his opinion of his boss, John Carter?

"He's a workaholic. He's tireless.

"The things you think he's going to be upset about, he isn't—and vice versa. He likes honesty. If a staff member goes to him and tells him they made a mistake, he is very understanding and kind.

"He's a great teacher. And he's been a good friend. His teaching methods inspire people and force people to think and to question error they may have been taught when growing up. I remember him saying, 'Don't go by what any pastor or priest says. Pick up a Bible and think for yourself. Go to Scripture and study.'"

Sandy Hou is more full of life than almost any woman you could meet. But unlike other effervescent people, she's able to concentrate for long periods of time. And she needs it. She is the video switcher when Carter's TV programs are recorded. That means she throws the switches to select which camera is being used. She must concentrate for an hour without a lapse, not for even one second. During most of her week, she does production work, such as helping edit videotapes to make completed *The Carter Report* TV programs.

"I love my job here," she says. "I think this is a wonderful work, not just for me, but for God.

"John Carter is a wonderful man, a wonderful preacher. He's very knowledgeable on what he preaches. I admire him because whenever he preaches, he focuses on the Bible. Not every pastor does that. He asks every person [in the audience] to open their Bibles when he preaches. I like to open the Bible because that is the source."

David Carter is John and Beverley's 40-year-old son. He works with his parents as the producer and director of the *Carter Report* TV program.

"Working in Russia changed my life," he says. "I had just graduated from Sydney College of the Arts at the University of Sydney. It was a very secular school and I was a cynical person. I had the fantasy of going to Art School in Moscow."

It didn't happen, and the first time he went to Russia it was for a totally different reason—as part of his father's TV crew. He was astonished to discover what a nation without God was like. "Witnessing what I witnessed in Russia changed me. When you get back home from Russia, you realise how trivial our problems are here."

David has insights that come only from being a family member.

While most people credit his father for the great success, David also looks in another direction. "If it weren't for my mum, I don't believe any of it would have happened. It's that simple. The old cliché 'behind every successful man . . .' is true in this case. A lot of people think she's nice, but mistake her niceness for weakness. She's not weak at all. She's very strong. Without her support, I don't believe anything would have happened in Russia."

David admires his father for "his tenacity, his drive and his vision. If he weren't driven so hard, all these things wouldn't have happened.

"I would say that Dad is the most recognised foreign minister in Russia."

However, in the day-to-day working environment, these two men are chalk and cheese. "Dad's not a technical person. He doesn't want to learn technical things. That's the biggest problem with Dad. He doesn't have a computer. He tends to think everything takes five minutes. It usually takes five days. He gets impatient when you try to explain things to him."

Misty Stiles, a businesswoman, purchased the Sky Angel satellite package looking for a TV alternative with less violence. She didn't know anything about 3ABN, which was part of the package. She was watching it for the first time when she saw a grey-haired man interviewing someone about the Reformation. She was annoyed when the grey-haired man said, "Christians don't know their faith." She thought that was an arrogant statement. Nonetheless, it spurred her to buy a historical book on the Reformation and use her university training to research the subject.

She was attending a non-denominational church that used the Bible in all its services. While there, she researched what the Bible had to say about the Sabbath. She came to the conclusion that Sunday was the wrong day. "I took my findings to the pastor, who politely dismissed them. He said the Sabbath had been done away with, but he couldn't give any evidence." That concerned her. Her church used the Bible, but couldn't use the Bible to explain why they didn't keep the Sabbath.

Then from researching her Bible, she discovered Christians should be evangelistic. Her church had no outreach projects, and the pastor didn't want any.

Misty picked up the *Yellow Pages* phone directory to try to find a church that met on Saturday. Her TV was turned to mute. But even though it was a worldwide TV network, at that very moment 3ABN put up the address of a Saturday-keeping church in Arcadia, just 30 minutes from her home. It was the same grey-haired guy. She felt it was "creepy" that the address came on the screen at the exact time she was looking up the *Yellow Pages*.

During the week a voice kept nagging her. So on Sabbath she visited John Carter's church in Arcadia. She asked the then-head elder Skip Kerekes, "Are you going to do anything weird today?"

He joked back, "Not today, you're safe."

Misty went to the internet to find out the core beliefs of the Seventh-day Adventist Church. She then researched each of those beliefs from the Bible. Carter gave her 100 videos, and she watched two or three tapes every day. She had found her spiritual home and was baptised.

Carter was impressed by Misty's business abilities. He asked her to work with him on the business side of his organisation. Her thoughts about Carter are through the eyes of an experienced businesswoman.

"I see him every day applying Christian principles to business. It's very refreshing. And it's unusual," she says. "I've found him to be very honest.

"And funny. He's a very funny guy. He's a genuine guy. What you see is what you get, and I like that.

"He seems to be really anchored in his faith. It truly guides his life. It seems to be the centre by which the man makes the decisions for his life. There hasn't been an occasion when I haven't seen him start by saying, 'Let's pray about it.' And it not only starts with prayer, it ends with it, regardless of the outcome—because he doesn't always get what he prays for. When we start with a prayer, you're hoping it goes a certain way. Yet when it doesn't work out the way you hoped it would have, he always closes with a prayer of thanks.

"He's also patient, which is unusual about a leader. So many leaders are so driven that they don't allow that patience. In the corporate world a guy who is driven will often push right past his people, giving them no time to grow. With Pastor Carter, he gives them a period of grace and allows them to come along in time.

"He has great clarity of thought. He sees things very much in black and white. I think it comes from his application of biblical standards. A thing is either right or it's wrong because of where he's pulling his standard from. And he will make references to that standard all the time.

"Some preachers will [merely] stand up on the stage and preach how to live. When John walks off the stage, he still lives it. I like that."

Daniel Burgos was raised an Adventist, but didn't know the gospel. If the gospel had been preached in his Spanish-language church, he couldn't remember it. "I understood the way of salvation to be legalistic. I knew myself and my failings—and knew I would never make it. So I said, 'Forget it. Why bother?'" At age 15, he gave up going to church.

Daniel had a cousin who had attended John Carter's Los Angeles meetings at the Shrine Auditorium. When he was 24, he met his cousin who said, "Come to my church. We have a great pastor, and it's a chance for you to meet the whole family."

Daniel went to church to see his relatives again. But he got more than he bargained for. "For the very first time in my life I heard the gospel. For the first time I really understood the gospel."

The third time he visited Carter's church, he could hardly believe how much God loved him. He just couldn't stop crying. Carter's preaching had changed his life.

Daniel was rebaptised and soon found himself teaching a Sabbath school class. Then he became the church's youth leader "and John Carter noticed my talents."

Carter wanted to pay for one of the church's young people to go on his next trip to Odessa. The young people themselves voted who it should be, and they chose Daniel.

After the Odessa series, Carter knew Daniel needed a job, and offered him maintenance work at *The Carter Report* office. These days Daniel prepares Carter's audiovisuals for his church services. And he accomplished the mammoth task of converting 1000 of Carter's archaeology photographs to digital format. This means the photos Carter uses for evangelism can be on a DVD, rather than 20 large slide carousels.

"I would consider Pastor Carter as my pastor and my friend, as well as my boss.

"He does a lot of work and he tends to let people know he's done a lot. He's proud to be a hard worker. A lot of us are concerned about that. We think he needs a break. He says he will take a break, but he never does.

"As a boss, what I like is that he acknowledges that you've done a good job. He's reinforcing the good traits in you. But he'll also let you know when you've made a mess of it.

"If there's any bad news, you don't tell him before he preaches. You don't want to frazzle him before a sermon. There's high tension before the first night of a campaign. You just say to John, 'Yes sir'; and you do what he says, and don't talk back. Sometimes you need a bit of thick skin [just before a series starts]."

Carter's staff have a strong sense that they are advancing the gospel by working for him. Daniel does too. But he also has an opposite feeling. "When I worked in a restaurant, I had more opportunities to talk to people [about God]. And I had more Bible studies [with non-Christians]."

Susan Piraino has worked for *The Carter Report* for 13 years. That's longer than anyone else except family members.

She was raised in an Adventist Church, but left when she was about 17 because she wasn't interested. She married a Catholic and had two children. It then started to haunt her that she wasn't giving her children Bible instruction. But she didn't do anything about it.

In April 1990, she saw TV advertising for meetings at the Shrine Auditorium in Los Angeles. Her Adventist mother suggested she attend. She went along to humour her mother.

"I was stunned. I was amazed. My mum had told me this guy is an Adventist, but he wasn't talking any Adventist theology. It wasn't your average type of church program. It was very professional, and I didn't associate that with the church."

Susan and her husband attended almost every night of the Shrine series for as long as it continued. Carter announced he was looking for a church where they could meet every Sabbath. Susan and her husband attended that church. And four months after they went to their first Shrine meeting, they were both baptised.

"As a preacher, John's the best I've ever heard," she says. "He's direct and to the point, clear and concise. When he goes through a doctrine or a text, it becomes clear. He's powerful in his preaching. He doesn't hold back. He tells it like it is, and that's nice for a change. It's not what I *want* to hear; it's what I *need* to hear.

"He knows how to bring secular people into the church."

Susan has a key role in *Carter Report* publicity. She prepares the reports that are regularly mailed to Carter's supporters. Carter writes the reports and suggests photos to include. But her artistic eye puts all the pieces together.

"He's very loyal," Susan says about her boss. "He's loyal to friends, to church members, and to anyone in the work environment. If he tells you he's going to do something, he's going to do it. If you have a problem, you can come to him and he'll help you resolve it.

"He doesn't give up—that's one of the things you have to admire about John. A lot of people would have walked away a long time ago if they had seen how difficult it was. He really perseveres. It's easy to say, 'I've done my share; I'm going to give up.' But he doesn't say that. I see him get discouraged, but then he turns around and keeps going."

What do most of the Carter team members have in common? They have spent a significant part of their adult life "in the world." Some have discovered the Adventist Church at the end of a spiritual journey. Most were raised Adventists, left the church, and then came back.

Obviously, these people do their jobs well but there is more to it than that. The mindset of the Carter team members is "We have been in the world. We have found it offers nothing. We have found the answers in the Bible and in the church. And we want to share those answers."

Right in the Middle of It

Bob Ludwig also fits the mould of Carter team members who left the church and came back. He is a member of the board of *The Carter Report, Inc.* He comes from a long line of Adventists, dating back to the 1890s. But when he was 12 years old, his parents divorced and he left the church.

Ludwig set up his own professional audio services business. He worked providing sound to some of the biggest names in the entertainment world. He did the audio work for the group Chicago on and off for 18 years. He's also provided the sound for Suzanne Somers, Michael Jackson, Seals and Crofts, and for three American presidents.

Then 23 years after he left, he started attending church again. At church he was given a brochure for meetings at the Shrine Auditorium.

That's a big hall, he thought to himself. *It seats 6000 people. I wonder if they need any help with their sound equipment.*

It took Ludwig only two phone calls to find John Carter's phone number. He introduced himself and told Carter about his work.

"You're an answer to prayer," Carter replied. Only days away from starting the Shrine meetings, he didn't have audio equipment or an audio operator.

"The next thing I know is that I was at the Shrine Auditorium and was due to mix the sound there for the next 30 days," says Ludwig.

"I was soaking up the program. I didn't even know John was a pastor. Then at the end of the second night, he prayed! I thought, *He's praying for 6000 secular people here in Los Angeles. What will they think?* I looked to see how people reacted. It was amazing to see 6000 people here in LA bow their heads in prayer. And I would say most of them were secular people. Certainly up to that point it was a secular event.

"From then on the program started with prayer and Bible study and it turned into more religious discussion. I was amazed because I had come out of the secular lifestyle just a year earlier. I knew a lot of people were not receptive to this. Even though the brochure said 'biblical archaeology' I focused on the 'archaeology' part. Naturally, some of the people dropped off after the first night. But a lot of people stayed on to see where this was headed, because John has a unique way of holding his audience's curiosity. The way he presents his information is that one thing leads to another thing the next night. When you learn this subject, you obviously want to learn about the next subject. I couldn't wait to get back the next day.

"This was a turning point for me and my walk. I had learned all the information as a child, but I had never connected the dots. John put all the pieces together. Then I felt I understood. I was 38 years old, and I had been taught these things from my earliest days in school. But now I saw the big picture."

Carter baptised Ludwig in the surf at the world-famous Malibu Beach. Just as Carter lowered him under the water, a huge wave came and rolled Ludwig all the way to the shore.

Five years later Carter asked Ludwig to do the audio work in Kiev, the capital city of Ukraine. He was heading for an extraordinary adventure.

"Kiev blew my mind. First of all, just going to the ex-Soviet Union was a big experience. At that time it had not yet Westernised completely."

Ludwig set up his sound mixers and control desk in the middle of the audience area. He tested all the equipment and the microphones. Everything was ready to go for the first meeting. Before the doors opened, someone said to him, "You should see the crowd outside."

So Ludwig grabbed his Nikon camera and walked up the stairs until he was about five storeys above the crowd. He looked through the giant glass panels and was astonished. "All I could see was a sea of people across the street and up the boulevard. There were people as far as I could see. There had to be tens of thousands. I didn't know how many. They later told me possibly 100,000. I was pumped with adrenaline. I had never seen anything like this in my life and I've done concerts with 200,000 people at them.

"I said to myself, *This is great! I've got to get more pictures of this.* So I went downstairs to the front doors. When I got there, the people were pushed up against the glass doors like sardines. They were packed. Then I started hearing glass break. The people were absolutely adamant about getting in. I took photos then thought, *I've got to get away from this before they open the doors to let the people in.*"

Ludwig realised the hall could hold only a small fraction of the crowd outside. Once they opened the doors, he expected bedlam. He knew that if he weren't at the sound mixing desk when the doors opened he wouldn't be able to get to the desk through the crowd.

"So I took my camera and went back to the mixing board, which was in the middle of the auditorium. Shortly after that they opened the doors and I heard thunder. The floor started shaking as people were running to get a seat. I was just shocked that these people were running and squeezing through every door they could get through. In a matter of minutes we had standing room only in this huge stadium. The people were crushing against me in the [sound] mixing area. There was no room in the aisles. I couldn't get out. I'm used to doing sound for crowds, but here I thought I might get killed. There would have been no way I could have made my way through the crowds to get to the mixer if I weren't there before the people rushed in.

"The building was already 100 degrees [40°C] inside before the people arrived. There was no air conditioning, so it then became extremely hot and sweaty. The locals don't take a lot of baths, so it was pretty smelly there."

About 12,500 people were crammed into a stadium with seating for 9500. It's estimated about 100,000 more people were still outside and couldn't get in. Ludwig's mind flashed back to the meetings in Los Angeles's Shrine Auditorium. Would these people react like the people did in LA? He felt that almost everyone in the Kiev audience was an atheist. What would their reaction be when Carter closed the meeting with prayer?

"When John prayed for them, it was interesting to watch more than 10,000 people who had never prayed before bowing their heads to pray. It was very moving. I had a sense of awe.

"John had gone to a country where he didn't speak the language, they didn't know him, they were atheists, and they knew nothing about the Bible. And yet he said a prayer for them and they all bowed their heads with him.

"He had to tell them what to do because they didn't know how to pray. It is such an awesome sight to see. For the first time I felt I was at the cutting edge of evangelism. You would never see this in America."

During the prayer two nights later, Carter asked those who wanted to become Christians to raise their hands. From where Ludwig sat in the middle of the stadium floor, it looked like every hand was raised.

He recalls that the next night John Carter had planned to make an altar call. That was an astonishing concept since the aisles were already crammed with people. How could the people possibly move forward?

"It was hard for them to move because it was so full. But they were all moving a little bit forward. It was amazing to watch because they were so hungry. The people hadn't experienced this before, and neither had a lot of us."

From where he sits Ludwig has a view of the meeting no-one else on the team has. He notices that the same people come to the same seats every night. It has become *their* seat.

For several nights Carter has been telling the people he would give them a free Bible if they attend for seven nights. Each night the people went to a desk near the front doors where the ushers marked an attendance card. But the decision was made that they would give a Bible to everyone here on the eighth night, even if they hadn't been to seven programs.

The crowds were now slightly smaller and there was room in the aisles. Before the crowds came in, the Carter team put stacks of Bibles in the aisles. More than 10,000 Bibles were stacked up for the 5 pm session. And as soon as the audience cleared, they put out stacks of another 10,000 Bibles for the 7 pm session.

"The piles of Bibles in the aisles were at least waist-high throughout the auditorium. The people came in and found their regular seats.

But they kept looking at the stacks of Bibles. They were thinking, *I'm going to get one of those. Today is the day.*

"We got to the point in the program where we were going to hand them out. The ushers came into the aisles and started passing out the Bibles. The people can't wait to get them. They open them up immediately and start reading. They finger through the pages as fast as they can. I could see couples and groups huddled together showing each other things in the Bible. It takes a lot to make me cry, but that night I shed a tear."

In these meetings, the Carter team gave out 30,000 Bibles. And because the people there speak two languages, they gave out Bibles in both Russian and Ukrainian. Ludwig noticed that the people held the Bibles close to their hearts like a valued possession.

Kiev was the first time Ludwig assisted with a Carter program in the former USSR. But he has been to every program there since. This first program set a pattern Ludwig has followed for each evangelistic series. He cannot stay for the full program because he has to run his business back in America. So during the first two weeks of Carter's meetings, he trains a local to do his job. After the second week of the program, he returns home to his business.

This means that at Kiev, Ludwig missed out on seeing the baptism. But, soon afterward, he went to *The Carter Report* office in California to watch a video of the baptism. And there he saw people he recognised being baptised. He didn't know their names—but he did know which seat they always sat in.

An interview with Willie Jordan

If the Protestant church had royalty, Willie Jordan would probably be the queen mother. She operates the Fred Jordan Mission, founded by her late husband to help people on skid row in Los Angeles. It cares for hungry, homeless and destitute people in America's inner cities. Jordan's TV program is on local stations in Los Angeles and San Francisco. It's on two satellites across America, and it's seen around the world. John Carter calls her one of the greatest preachers in the world.

Jordan is so astute in evangelism and so highly respected she was one of 12 people on the Billy Graham Crusade committee in LA. And while she and Carter are from different religious denominations, she also sits on the board of *The Carter Report, Inc.* She has been to the former USSR with the Carter team and was astonished by what she saw.

What was your impression of the Carter crusade?

I was amazed at the reception of the people when John stood up to preach. It was just beautiful to see thousands of people almost walk over the people in front of them to get inside. Each evening he had two sessions. It was wonderful to see their hearts open.

What did you think about the reaction of the people?

I'll never forget the first service there in Kharkov in the Ukraine. At the close of the service, John basically said, "You have been taught there is no God. But if there *is* a God, would you like Him to help you? Do you have any needs?" These are people who had never heard the Word of God, who had never heard of prayer. And the people stood.

Right across the aisle from me was a young woman in her early 20s. Big tears rolled down her cheeks as she raised her hands [to show she wanted prayer]. I looked around and saw similar reactions on the faces of other people. It touched my heart beyond belief. That same thing happened night after night. And as I realised where I was standing, in what used to be the Soviet Union, to see this response was overwhelming.

What do you think of John's method of reaching secular and atheistic people?

I think it's wonderful. He's very pragmatic. He goes into history. And for people who have really no concept of God, this is a wonderful way to reach them. If you went there and said, "God loves you; He sent His Son Jesus," they would say, "Well, who is God?" So I think his approach is a wonderful way to reach secular people, many of whom are well educated. This appeals to them. And obviously the results, those who come forward for salvation and those who are baptised, show how valuable this approach is and how it really does work.

What is your personal opinion of John Carter?

I've been around a long time. I'm older than John. I have been in ministry well over 50 years. And I have not often met men of God who have [John's] integrity. You know that what he says is coming from his heart. You know that he's going to be a man of his word. And I have known him long enough to know this is true. The passion for the lost is what appeals to me about John Carter. The bottom line is bringing people to the bottom of the cross to find salvation. And this is John's entire motivation, as I have seen it and watched his ministry.

What would you say is John's greatest strength?

He is bold. John Carter is not afraid of the devil and all his antics. John Carter boldly proclaims the gospel. John is not affected by what men think. He is not deterred by men's negativity. John is committed to preaching the Word. And he will do that regardless. And that is rare today.

What would you say is his greatest weakness?

That he thinks he can do it all. His body can't keep up with his passion for souls. That is probably his greatest weakness. But as long as God continues to give him strength, I can't find fault with this.

You sit on the board of **The Carter Report***. What is John like in board meetings?*

He is very straightforward in what he feels God has called him to do. And I believe God has blessed him with a board that also truly believes in the vision. The reason I am on his board is that I believe his vision is God-given.

John is very clear [as a chairman]. He is not wishy-washy. He presents what he feels God wants him to do, and then we discuss how to help him. I believe that this is a board member's responsibility on any board, and especially in ministry. First, you have to believe in the leader, and in the vision God has given him or her. And when he lays out the vision, I believe it's our responsibility as board members to facilitate that vision becoming reality. So I am thrilled to be part of John Carter's ministry and part of *The Carter Report*.

How well does the Carter program compare to Billy Graham's?

I would say they compare [equally] in their passion for the lost, but John certainly does it a lot cheaper! [*Willie laughs.*] For dollars spent, I'm amazed. I couldn't believe in the Ukraine how little was expended for the numbers of people who came to Jesus. And that's a very practical thing that all of us in ministry have to look at—because there are not dollars to do everything we want. The dollars are not unlimited. But John is very careful, I would say he is probably tight, in the way he spends money. And so you get a lot of results for every dollar.

You watched the Ukraine program. What were its strengths?

One of the main things that impressed me was the way they went out to the people. They had advertising on the sides of the buses and trams. That was a very effective way to reach out to the people. So the expenditure of money was well done. He used radio and television also.

It is more than successful when people break down the doors to get in! And to force you to have two meetings each night shows the effectiveness of how they spent the money.

What improvements would you like to see? What were the weaknesses?

That's a hard question because I wouldn't even presume to change anything. What I saw was working. And when I say "working," that means souls coming to the Lord. That was very effective. I wouldn't change anything.

You're a television evangelist, as John is. As one of his peers, how to you rate John Carter's television program?

Oh, I think it's great. I think his sincerity is one of the greatest things that comes across. In a huge public arena, you can hear it. And with a television camera, you can see it. You can see that he has one goal—and that is to present to you the claims of Jesus Christ and the salvation that He offers. That is a real winner on the television front.

Is there anything else you'd like to say about John Carter?

I would like to say that John is one of the good guys—really. I firmly believe in what God has called him to do. I am honoured to call John Carter a friend. And more honoured to have John call me a friend. You'll have to look long and hard to find someone who supports John more than I do. He's special. And of course, his wife, Beverley, she is a dear.

Tell me about Beverley.

I love Beverley because she supports her husband. I think for a wife of a man in ministry, the greatest thing she can do is love and support and back her husband to facilitate all that God has called him to do. And I see this in Beverley. And frankly, I don't see it in a lot of wives of preachers and evangelists. They somehow feel they need to be in the public eye, to be recognised. But Beverley is not that way.

Some people close to the Carters believe John would be nothing like the success he has been without Beverley.

Oh, I agree with that! [*Willie laughs.*] This is too much of a burden for one person to carry. So a pastor can't do it without that support. And Beverley is John's stability. She is behind him. And if people disagree with him, she's there to assure him. I think there's nothing like a couple working together. I love to see John and Beverley. Their love and respect for one another is tremendous.

Do you think we will ever see another John Carter?

I don't think so. There is a whole different feeling out there among the young people in our churches. I was 13 when I committed my life to the Lord. And the church then had an environment that encouraged that. Throughout my youth and into my twenties I would hear pastors and evangelists encourage [young people] to give their lives to full-time ministry as a missionary, a local pastor or whatever. I don't hear that today. I haven't heard it for many years. So young people today don't see the value of ministry. But is there value in doing anything other than ministry?

We won't see another John. But I pray your book will be used to encourage young people to strive to be used as John has been used.

THE JOHN CARTER
YOU DON'T SEE

Aperson's public life is just the tip of the iceberg. Far more is not seen than is seen. So what is the real John Carter like—the one the public does not see?

Possibly the first secret is that he doesn't have many hobbies. He likes classical music concerts, but he lives so far from downtown Los Angeles he attends only one every second year. He watches TV, but not a huge amount. He doesn't play golf or go to sporting events.

Perhaps the closest thing to a hobby Carter has is his car. "I love to polish my car," he says.

"He is meticulous about caring for his car," says one of his fellow ministers.

And another minister says, "He always washes his car as if he's about to sell it."

"He is a hard worker as far as housekeeping is concerned. He waters the garden and cuts the lawn himself. He even vacuum-cleans the house," says a colleague.

Carter is not skilled in manual tasks, says a pastor who lived next door to him when his children were young. "I helped John put up a swimming pool," he says. "Among John's many talents is not one for putting up pools—or even for looking after one."

On one occasion Carter was trying to clean the above-ground pool and it collapsed. A wall of water ran down toward the road, with only the house of the pastor next door standing in its way. When the wave hit the neighbour's house, water flew high into the air. "I'm not very good at things like that," he confesses.

Carter likes still photography—but it probably isn't a hobby. His organisation produces magazines and newsletters for supporters each month, and he takes most of the photos used in the magazines. His evangelistic meetings feature as many as 100 photos each night, most of which he has taken himself.

He could have arranged a large salary from his organisation, and then bought an expensive home near his office in Los Angeles. But he hasn't. In fact, because houses in Los Angeles cost so much, he purchased a house in Thousand Oaks, where the real estate was cheaper. Ironically, that cost-saving measure means time-conscious Carter spends about 12 hours a week driving to and from his office.

"Everything in his house is very practical," says a friend who's been a house guest. "He lives simply and doesn't have the elements of luxury in his home. But he has a lot of souvenirs of Russia."

His office is not especially large. It has nothing of the luxury one may imagine a successful TV presenter might have. The main wall is simply cement brick painted light blue. The room is utilitarian rather than luxurious. His glass-topped wooden desk is only a moderate size. A bookcase contains about 150 books, most of them on religious themes. He has six different translations of the Bible within easy reach of his desk.

A bonsai plant sits on his desk, as does a globe of the world with a grey stetson hat perched on it—perhaps a reminder of his earlier days in Texas. Also on his desk is a replica of King Tut's face mask, and two models of classic American cars: a Pontiac GTO and a Chevrolet Chevele SS454.

Hanging on the wall are several award certificates his *Carter Report* TV program has won. There are two pictures of Sydney Harbour showing the famous Sydney Opera House, where he held an evangelistic series. And dominating the wall is an advertising sign for Australian-made products someone has framed. It reads "Fair dinkum. Aussie made. Aussie owned."

Possibly Carter's most significant extravagance is to have a second house in Australia. He financed it by mortgaging his home in California. Both homes are on the edge of the city so he can take his walks each day in natural surroundings.

On his daily walks John prays, thinks about the beauty of nature, and considers what he is going to preach. "I have heaps of sermon [ideas] running around my head crying, 'Let me out! Preach me!'" he explains. "From all these thoughts, I select a topic on Monday or Tuesday. I cogitate on it for a few days, start writing some notes about Thursday, and then do a final outline on Friday night."

"John finds it hard to relax. He is always on the go," says one of his friends. "If he were a horseman, he would sleep in the saddle and keep riding so he didn't waste time."

Carter is also a good TV scriptwriter, but he doesn't do it often. Among his writing was the script of the 1992 award-winning TV documentary *Victory at Gorky*. He writes his own monthly fundraising letters to his supporters—no ghostwriters here.

At his office, Carter's office staff wear casual clothes, but he always wears a suit and tie. His dress sense is more European than

Australian or American. The exception to this is that he wears short boots rather than shoes—again, it's possibly a Texas influence.

John and Beverley begin their mornings together with worship in John's study. He reads a Bible passage and they both pray. They also have personal worship time separately.

Carter eats a healthy breakfast. "He has the best eating habits of anyone I know. Out of all the Adventists I know, he is one of the best observers of health reform," says a fellow minister.

And he doesn't smoke. He never drinks alcohol. He doesn't even drink mildly damaging drinks like tea and coffee. He believes we should "purge ourselves from all that contaminates body and mind" (see 2 Corinthians 7:1).

Carter's sister, Margaret Morrissey, describes him as being "absolutely sincere. He believes every word he says. I think he is the most dedicated, conscientious person I know."

Carter has two high-definition TV sets in his home. If you find him watching TV, the set will probably be tuned to the Discovery Channel, the History Channel or news.

He also reads a lot. You can talk to him on a wide range of topics and his comments will always be up to date. He regularly reads *National Geographic, Time, Business Week,* and *US News and World Report*, plus an occasional car magazine. If friends find a significant article in a magazine he doesn't read, they will clip out the article for him. What he reads in these magazines often finds its way into his sermons. "I like my preaching to be in touch with what's going on in the world," he says.

He reads a lot about science. A book about science and religion will often be in his briefcase. And he reads a lot of history.

But, most significantly, he is a great Bible reader. His most frequent message to his church members is, "Read your Bible every day." He reads his Bible devotionally each morning and finishes his day with the Bible. One pastor says, "I have seen John at the end of the day so tired he was almost falling to the floor. However, he still read his Bible before going to sleep." And if he wakes up during the night, he again reads his Bible.

Carter is deeply affected by people's misfortune. "Whenever there is trouble, John is always there to help," says one Russian church pastor. "He's helped many people in Russia who have cancer or hepatitis C, and people threatened by the Mafia. One church member was about to be killed by the Mafia, so John paid his debt to save his life. John provides cancer victims with money for surgery. He is always a great help to people in trouble. As soon as he is aware of a problem, he offers help first—then he asks the details of the problem."

"John has the rare ability to think big," says a minister who worked on Carter's team for the evangelistic series at Sydney Opera House. "Plus he is able to raise the money to carry out his seemingly impossible aspirations. And finally he delivers the goods."

John Carter was a role model for a generation of Adventist ministers in Russia. When the Iron Curtain fell and religious freedom was granted by law, Protestant churches started booming. However, there were not enough ministers. The Christian Adventist Church rushed new ministers into the field while they completed their studies by correspondence. Many of these novice pastors assisted in his evangelistic series. It was valuable training. "John taught the Russian ministers who worked with him a high sense of responsibility," says one Russian church president.

"I have great respect for him as a person, as a Christian and as an evangelist. I would call him the best Adventist evangelist in the world," says another leading evangelist. "There is no-one in the USA, South America or Europe who is better than him. Dick Barron in the United States is the only one who comes close to John in dynamics and capturing the audience's attention. John is a big-audience preacher. We have a lot of good preachers, but not a lot we can put into a big stadium."

"People like John because he's a real man," says a Russian pastor. "He is not effeminate. He is masculine. The reason why John won the Russian hearts is that he is a real man. He's not a cat; he's a tiger. Russians like strong men."

If Carter is at an airport between planes, he doesn't waste the waiting time. He goes for a walk. And he even counts the steps so he knows how far he has walked.

On one occasion the temperature was 38 degrees below zero. That temperature can kill people, but Carter wanted to walk, so he took two Russian ministers with him. It was too cold for even Russian people to be on the streets. But he set a brisk pace down the street for an hour-long walk—with his two unwilling companions.

SOME VERY IMPRESSIVE PEOPLE

D uring his time working in Russia, John Carter has worked with many impressive people. They range from the most humble to the most senior. Let's meet some of these impressive people.

"Paul the Prisoner"

One impressive man Carter calls "Paul the Prisoner." During the Communist era, he had a secret printing press hidden in his basement. He published Christian literature for a church starving for the printed word. He was able to run his secret printing operation for years. But then a traitor in the church reported him to the KGB.

Paul earned his name "the Prisoner" because of what the KGB did to him. They put him in what is called a "refrigerator cell." That is where the temperature in the cell is deliberately kept only a degree or two above freezing. They gave him only one meal a day so his body did not have enough food to generate body heat. And they kept him there for three years.

When Communism collapsed, Paul was released from prison.

But he still had printer's ink in his veins. He still wanted to publish God's message.

When Carter was a pastor in Australia, he had written material for young people in his church called *The Big Issues of the Gospel*. This booklet showed that we are saved by faith. Paul was impressed by this book and he arranged for it to be translated it into Russian.

Another of Paul's projects was to print a large book based on Carter's 26-meeting evangelistic campaigns. Each chapter of *Amazing Discoveries* is from a transcript of a night of Carter's meetings, translated into a beautiful standard of Russian. Printing *Amazing Discoveries* has been an expensive project. He printed 20,000 with funds donated by *The Carter Report*. But Paul's ambition is to print a million copies of *Amazing Discoveries* and spread them across Russia. All he needs is the money.

Alexander Antonyuk

Another impressive person is Pastor Alexander Antonyuk. He was the president of the largest Adventist local conference in the former USSR. Despite this large area to supervise, Alexander was an evangelist. He felt he had a more important work to do than being an administrator. He spent so much time preaching that other church leaders felt he wasn't paying enough attention to administration. So he was replaced as president.

No longer an administrator, Alexander had more time to be an evangelist. He is now sponsored by *The Carter Report, Inc* and he runs about six evangelistic programs a year. Each baptises about 200 people. And he does it almost single-handedly.

Even as a child, Alexander was true to God. School in Russia ran six days a week, but young Alexander wanted to obey the Ten

Commandments, so he missed school every Sabbath. When he came to school on Monday, the teacher would make him put his fingers on the desk and beat them mercilessly with a fibreglass ruler.

When he was 19 and was conscripted into the army, he decided he would still keep the Sabbath. To break his will, he was put on duty for 24 hours on Sabbath. But he refused to do it. He was punished by being put on duty 48 hours *straight*. He was then thrown in jail. Eventually, they offered to let him out and make him a captain in the KGB. All he had to do was inform on church members. He didn't accept the offer.

After being discharged from the army, he became a pastor. But under Russian law, he also had to work full time in secular work. It was illegal to pay wages to a Protestant minister. If the pastor missed 15 days doing his secular work, he was put in prison. Every time he got a job, the KGB ordered he be sacked. He was sacked 11 times in 1984 alone as the KGB tried to create a situation where he would miss 15 days work. And all that time Alexander was preaching the gospel.

Alexander now ranks as one of the most successful evangelists in the former USSR. Most of Alexander's series are financed by *The Carter Report*. He is normally the master of ceremonies for the Carter campaigns. And after Carter's meetings, he holds an hour-long question-and-answer session for those who want more information.

When Carter ran his second major series in Russia, Alexander was team manager. Carter was impressed by what he calls Alexander's "outstanding administration," and he has been manager for every Russian and Ukraine Carter series since, except one. He brings all his extraordinary skills as a church administrator to his role. He is in charge of almost everything, except what the preacher says.

"Alexander is the best negotiator I have met anywhere in the world," says Carter. "If you want something at the right price, you send Alexander. If he can't do it, nobody can. He has a charming personality. He could sell ice-cream to an Eskimo."

Alexander's position as the meeting's manager is vital because it takes pressure off the preacher. All Carter has to concern himself with his what he will say. Staff don't worry Carter with minor problems; Alexander handles that. While it is a thankless job, unseen by the public, it ranks with the preacher and the translator as among the most important tasks. If the manager does a poor job, the series will be a disaster. That Carter's series have been so successful is testament to Alexander's work.

Alexander works with each series for as long as nine months. Once the program is over, he puts on the hat of a senior church pastor, caring for new converts and guiding the pastors in setting up the new churches.

Many people need more than a month to make a decision for Christ. So Carter organises further meetings for these people to attend after he is gone. The programs are called Revelation Seminars and they are led by Pastor Alexander. Alexander and the local churches usually baptise 300-400 more people after Carter has gone.

President with a vision

The late Pastor Bjarne Christensen was a godly man who was the president of the Adventist Church in Southern California. It is a full-time duty. Christensen was engrossed in his work and was committed to the people of Southern California.

One of the church pastors in his administrative area was John Carter. Some were claiming that Carter wasn't totally committed to Southern California. He kept being distracted by his vision of Russia.

Shortly after Christensen was elected president of the Southern California Conference, he called Carter into his office to dismiss him.

"The committee thinks your work is of no value," Christensen told Carter. "I'm afraid you're sacked."

"I refuse to be sacked," Carter told him.

The president appeared confused. "The committee says you have to go."

"I have a higher authority than the committee," Carter replied.

"What's that?" Christensen asked.

"It's my local congregation. I will call a meeting of the church and tell the congregation I've been sacked."

"We don't want you to tell anybody," Christensen replied. "We want you to go back to Australia and go quietly."

The Carter Report's lawyer was at their meeting. By coincidence he was also a long-time friend of Christensen. He joined the conversation by indicating to Christensen that dismissing John Carter would result in significant controversy for the church. Such an outcome would not serve Christensen or Carter.

Carter and his lawyer left the president's office and Carter called a meeting of his congregation. The congregation voted to form *The Carter Report, Inc* to be a tax-exempt company that would allow Carter to continue his work. This was to be one of the most important decisions of Carter's life.

On the other side of the debate, the Southern California Conference administrative committee also met to try to resolve the developing crisis. But something was happening to Christensen. As he investigated the issues further, he changed his mind about Carter and now became his advocate. Other members of the conference committee also started to see the value of Carter's work.

A few weeks later, Christensen phoned Carter following a meeting that had gone late into the night. "You can remain as a pastor in Southern California," he told Carter. "The committee has also agreed to your independent ministry, but we want two representatives on *The Carter Report* company board."

Carter agreed (although it was later found to be illegal to have representatives from one 501(c)(3) company on the board of another). The situation was resolved and from this difficult situation came two huge positive steps. Carter's local church set up the tax-exempt company that became the organisation to evangelise the former USSR. And Christensen became one of Carter's closest friends—and one of the strongest advocates for his work in Russia.

"This gives people confidence in the church," Carter said later. "We can argue and we can disagree. However, from our disagreements we get a good outcome. Paul and Barnabus had a few disagreements and that's in the Bible.

"If we become 'yes men,' we sell our souls," Carter said.

Carter invited Christensen to join the team on his next visit to Russia. As he saw what was happening at Carter's meetings, the spirit of evangelism was rekindled in his soul. Christensen was particularly impressed when he visited the KGB training college and heard Carter defend Christianity to 1000 KGB trainees.

"Going to Russia changed my life," he told Carter.

A few years later, Christensen again went to Russia. This time he was the organiser of Carter's Trans-Siberian Express trip. His management expertise was a major reason the project was so successful.

Christensen had caught a vision that "this good news about the kingdom will be proclaimed all over the world" (see Matthew 24:14).

And he kept his vision of taking the gospel to all the world until his premature death, aged 51.

Billy Graham's organist

For six years, Carter's organist in the former USSR was Paul Mickelson. If you type his name into an internet search engine, you will immediately see his impact on 50 years of religious music.

From 1950 to 1957, Paul played the organ for the Billy Graham crusades. That made Paul the organist for two of the most important evangelistic programs in history—the 1954 Greater London Crusade and the 1957 Greater New York Crusade. Both programs ran for about 100 days.

Mickelson brought the song "How Great Thou Art" to the United States. Paul's playing accompanied the singing of the renowned George Beverly Shea hundreds of times.

Reader's Digest voted Paul one of the Top 10 organists in America. He produced Pat Boone's first album. When only 29 years old, Paul became vice-president of Word Records. He was a conductor of the Concert Orchestra of London. He knew 3000 hymns by heart. He produced many albums of his own music, as well as producing albums for some of the greatest names in religious recording. He published sheet music of his own original compositions for instruments as varied as the trumpet and the flute. The fine print on many 33 and 45 rpm religious recordings reads, "Paul Mickelson Orchestra and Choir."

At first, Paul's association with Carter was purely professional. Commencing in 1991, he was a paid organist for *Carter Report* programs, both in the United States and the former USSR.

In 1995, Paul played the organ for Carter's series in Kiev. "I have never seen anything like this, not even in the Billy Graham crusades," Paul said. "This is a greater response than anything we saw in any Billy Graham program. Billy's programs do not have large numbers like these coming down to the front."

"It was such a blessing for Paul to see 10,000 to 20,000 people raise their hand to accept Christ," Paul's wife, Barbara, recalls. "And it thrilled Paul when he saw 3500 people baptised in the Dnieper River. To him, it was like a second Pentecost."

When he returned from Kiev, Paul wrote original music for Carter's award-winning TV documentary *Victory at Kiev*.

Later that same year John held an evangelistic series in Pasadena, 16 kilometres (10 miles) from the centre of Los Angeles. Again, Paul was the organist—but he was no longer attending in just a professional capacity. He carefully listened to every word preached. He had never heard anything like Carter and his message. Carter's Pasadena series lifted Paul to a new spiritual plateau. He and Barbara decided to be baptised again and to join the Seventh-day Adventist Church. Carter personally baptised them.

Being Carter's organist reminded Paul of his early years with Billy Graham. Paul's adult life had started and was about to end playing the same role. In 2001, he died of a heart attack, aged 73.

Paul was in a unique position. He had played the organ for two of the world's greatest evangelists. It was natural for him to draw comparisons between the two. His assessment was that "John Carter is Billy Graham's successor."

THE "MARTIN LUTHER" OF RUSSIA

There is a man John Carter calls the "Martin Luther" of Russia. His name is Vadim Butov.

In Carter's second year at Gorky, he gave a series of seminars to 40 pastors who were helping him run his program. Each of the seminars was about the gospel. Though he was a trainee pastor, 17-year-old Vadim was confused about salvation. But as Carter taught them about God's free grace, Vadim says, "It was as though the windows of heaven opened."

Carter says there is probably not a stronger advocate for God's grace in the whole of Russia. Vadim frequently holds gospel meetings and evangelistic campaigns. These have baptised almost 8000 people.

Vadim took over the role as John's translator at the St Petersburg series. He has been Carter's translator ever since. Carter believes Vadim will replace him as the most successful evangelist in Russia. Vadim's work is now sponsored by the viewers of *The Carter Report* TV program.

When Vadim first became Carter's translator, the pair would spend an hour before each meeting going through the proposed sermon.

Now, because Vadim knows the material so well, the briefings are only five to 10 minutes. They just discuss new points in the presentation. With Carter's form of preaching, the translator cannot stop to think. He has to have a quick reaction time when Carter finishes his sentence. Without the briefing session beforehand, this style of preaching would be impossible.

Many preachers allow their translators to paraphrase their words. Carter, however, wants a precise translation. Once at St Petersburg he used the word *Communism*, but Vadim said "atheism" in his translation. Carter realised this because in this instance the Russian and English words sound similar. So he walked behind his translator, prodded him in the back, and whispered, "I said *Communism!*" Vadim corrected his translation.

When he preaches, Carter uses a lot of English idioms and proverbs that cannot be directly translated into Russian. So before a Carter campaign starts, Vadim reads a volume of Russian poetry to boost his active vocabulary. Then when Carter uses an English idiom, Vadim may have a Russian idiom available to say in its place. For example, if John wants people to remember something, he might say, "Let these words sink into your minds." Vadim could convey the same idea with the Russian idiom, "Put this on your moustache."

Some preachers write out their sermons in full and memorise them. Others write them out in full and read them. Carter usually writes only an outline. He knows the general direction his sermon will go, but the actual words are decided at the actual time.

Vadim says Carter's unplanned scripts make it more difficult for a translator. While he finds it easier translating for other preachers, he prefers doing the hard work translating for Carter.

Vadim says a translator for Carter needs to be accurate. But he must also speak in a way that is literary—or to use his term, in a way "that is tasty to the Russian ear."

He says that, as a translator, he must convey Carter's emotions, as well as his words. He has to be Carter's duplicate. He must be invisible. He has to make the people think Carter is speaking Russian.

Because of Vadim's translating skills, it is not a disadvantage for Carter to be speaking in a foreign language. In fact, his preaching is more powerful when he works with a translator than when he preaches to an English-speaking audience. Possibly it's the camaraderie of having someone on the stage with him. Possibly it's because every three seconds he has a pause to think about his next words. Or maybe it's because he speaks for only half the amount of time (the translator is taking the other half of the time). So he leaves less important details out of his sermon.

Hearing spoken English was a reason some people came to his meetings in Russia. People who had learned English at school could come and hear someone speaking it. And if Carter used English words they didn't know, the translator would interpret it three seconds later. It was a good way for Russians to brush up on their English. Hundreds of people were baptised who came along to hear the English language—and in the process, heard the gospel.

Vadim Butov was born in 1976 into an atheistic home. Both of his grandfathers were punished by the Communists by being expelled to the Southern Ural area of Russia. This meant there was little love for Communism in his home. His parents tried to educate him well so that one day he could leave Russia. As part of that process, he was taught English. He was reading the works of William Shakespeare when he was only 11 years old.

His family was poor, but he believed poverty was a noble thing. He still has almost no desire for material things.

One day he asked his grandmother, "What would happen if I read the Bible?" She replied, "Grandson, never do that. You will go mad." She was also afraid he would go to jail.

Young Vadim loved to read history books and encyclopedias. When he was about 13, he found the subject "Bible mythology" in an encyclopedia. He wrote down all the names of the "mythological" characters, creating a genealogy. Around the same time he found a book criticising the first 11 chapters of Genesis. Spread through the book's 700 pages were all the verses of those 11 chapters. He found each one, wrote them out in order, and memorised the 11 chapters. These were his earliest ventures into religion.

"Like all people, I was really afraid of death. I hated funerals. As atheists, we knew that this was the end."

Vadim wanted to become a lawyer or a diplomat. He never thought religion would be a significant part of his future. But when he was 14, the world as he knew it came to an end. In 1990, freedom came to Russia. The Soviet Government passed laws granting religious liberty.

"My mother took me to the Russian Orthodox Church and I was baptised by sprinkling. My mother had been secretly baptised by the Orthodox Church as a baby. It's an interesting fact that most atheists in the Soviet Union were baptised as babies in case there *was* a god.

"After I was baptised into the Orthodox Church, my parents thought I would forget about it, like most people do. But I took it seriously and secretly attended the Orthodox Church. The thing I liked most about it was confessing my sins to the priest and hearing him say, 'Vadim, your sins are forgiven.'"

At the start of the school year in September 1991, a teacher told him about a program in the school's 700-seat drama theatre. It was called "Evenings with the Bible." It was a five-day evangelistic campaign by Seventh-day Adventists. "I came to those meetings and I received a lot of pleasure from the preaching. But at the same time I was jealous that it was not the Orthodox Church that was taking the meetings. On the last day I said to a classmate who came with me, 'I will never become a Seventh-day Adventist.' Then I developed an aim to study the Bible well enough to prove Adventism wrong.

"I didn't have enough money to buy a Bible. In those days a Bible cost the equivalent of two months salary. So I went to the library to read the Bible and look for texts to prove the Adventists wrong."

At this time, Vadim was training to win a boxing title in his province. Winning this was important to him and most people expected him to take the title. However, a few months earlier he had been to a training camp and a stray punch caused him severe earache. He prayed, "God, if you heal my ear, I am prepared to lose the title." His pain soon vanished.

A few days before the championship he wanted to break his agreement with God but when he walked into the ring, he could barely move his arms. It was too easy for his opponent, who defeated Vadim by a technical knockout. Vadim left the ring greatly humiliated. He was upset and in anger said, "God, I don't believe You exist."

Vadim continued to study the Bible to prove the Adventists wrong but his research wasn't producing the results he expected. Three months after the meetings in the school theatre, he began to think he should attend the Adventist Church. He found out Adventists were selling Bibles for only two weeks wages, so he decided to buy one from them. And after school on Saturday, December 18, 1991, he went to the Adventist Church to buy the Bible. Vadim remembers the date well.

"I went to the church and purchased the Bible. The pastor's wife came outside with me. It was 30 below zero [-34°C]. She asked me a question. 'Vadim, what would you like to become in the future?' I said, 'A lawyer or a diplomat.' She hardly knew me, but she asked, "Vadim, don't you want to become a pastor of our church? Don't you think the Lord is calling you to become a minister?' There was so much warmth in my heart from those words. I kept talking to her for two hours and she always answered from the Bible.

"After we finished talking, I went home by bus. I said to myself, 'I will become a Seventh-day Adventist and I *will* become a minister of this church.' The change happened in two hours. I opened my new Bible and it smelled so nice. I set a goal to read the Bible in 66 days—a book of the Bible each day. I decided to memorise Bible texts as much as I could."

Vadim started attending the Adventist Church, which meant skipping school on Saturdays. However, Vadim was capable of an A-level performance even if he missed a day of school each week. In his final exams he received an "A" in every subject except one. One teacher, furious about him missing Saturdays, deliberately marked him down to a "B."

"My English teacher said, 'Vadim, are you sure Adventism is right?' So I promised her I would talk to the priests and pastors of every religious group I could find in my city and ask them questions from the Bible." Despite his deep and widespread inquiries, he found nothing that suggested he was taking the wrong path.

On May 29, 1992, 16-year-old Vadim was baptised, just a week before John Carter's first baptism on Russian soil.

Vadim set himself an aim: by the end of the year—seven months away—he wanted to talk to 1500 people about Christ. He talked to people at school, on public transport or wherever he met them. And he kept a diary to record how many conversations he had. "By the end of the year I had personally spoken to 2000 people."

In Russian schools, every boy is seated next to a girl. One of the people he spoke to was the girl he sat next to. She told him emphatically, "Vadim, I will never attend your church!"

Vadim replied, "Anna, let me prophesy. In a few years, you and your mother and your brother will all be members of our church."

Two years later, her brother was baptised. Three years later, her mother was baptised. And seven years later, Vadim returned to that city as an evangelist, and he personally baptised Anna. She is now one of the most active church members in her city.

This evangelistic series was held in the same school's 700-seat theatre where Vadim attended his first Adventist meetings. The hall was packed for three sessions each day and 505 people were baptised.

Evangelism has become progressively more expensive in Russia and *The Carter Report* continues to sponsor Vadim's evangelistic programs, including providing funds for the purchase of Bibles.

But finance is not the only thing Vadim gets from Carter. He also receives advice. "He's a great counsellor. He often can prevent me from making mistakes because he has done these things before in his life," says Vadim.

"For example, in 1997 I was appointed the regional youth director for the church. After two weeks I went to St Petersburg to translate for John. In the hotel room, John held my head with both hands, then said [about my head], 'There doesn't seem to be anything wrong with it. So why would you leave evangelism?' After two months I resigned and went back to conference evangelism. In the next two years I baptised 1800 people."

Today, Vadim has personally started 31 new churches, and helped Carter start dozens more. He has a giant intellect and speaks half a dozen languages. At home, he reads the New Testament in the original Greek.

The Russian university that trains Adventist ministers wants him on staff. But rather than have the life of an academic, he wants to remain an evangelist. Yet he does give the future ministers one month a year. He teaches three subjects at the seminary: "Pastoral Theology," "Public Evangelism" and "The Art of Speech." These courses are all crammed into 28 days. He gives six to nine lectures a day in intensive courses to second- and third-year ministerial students.

RECORDING CARTER'S TV PROGRAM

John Carter's TV program is one of the highest rating shows on the worldwide 3ABN TV network. His programs are also shown worldwide on Hope-TV and Safe-TV. He's been on religious TV every week since he started his TV program in Texas in 1987.

Carter's TV show appeals to the intellectuals, but also to the simple, exploring mind-stretching themes, but in simple ways.

Some of his TV programs are recorded in Russia. Occasionally some come from Egypt, Australia or Israel. But the largest percentage are broadcasts of meetings at his church in California. The idea of televising his sermons was a suggestion by his wife, Beverley.

Carter's church building—Community Adventist Fellowship in Arcadia, California—looks like any other church but it's actually a giant TV studio. At first glance one doesn't notice anything different. However, looking closely at the walls one can see they have sound-deadening panels to stop sound bouncing off the walls and creating a "hollow" sound when the program is recorded. One professional singer says the acoustics and PA here make this church the best place she has sung in anywhere in the world.

Another thing that's different from a normal church is a TV camera crane. It sits permanently at the front of the church. When the sermon is televised, three other cameras are in the congregation. All the cabling for the cameras is permanently built in. Huge banks of studio floodlights are built into the ceiling. And a building next door is equipped with the full array of broadcast production equipment.

Today, we arrive about 8.15 am, three hours before the recording will begin. The car park is almost empty. But several cars have been parked here for almost an hour. The top technical people are already hard at work. Within a few minutes several more cars arrive. These are the four camera operators. Each cameraman not only takes the pictures; he does the skilled task of setting up the camera he will use.

The cameras are positioned about halfway between the front and the rear of the church. One is being positioned in the middle, one at the right, and one at the left. The fourth camera is being placed on the crane. It swings from the right-hand edge to almost the middle of this wide room. And it rises high in the air to take elevated shots.

Each camera is readied, plugged in and switched on. The technicians run a series of tests to ensure each is operating perfectly.

Two large TV control rooms are in the building next door. One room controls the sound, the other the picture. In the audio control room the operators check the day's program sheet. It says Carter will conduct an interview as part of his worship program. That means he will have two microphones, one in his hand, the other attached to his coat. He will sound slightly different in each microphone. The audio control room staff will record each microphone onto separate tapes. That will allow the editors to select his voice from either microphone if the difference in sound quality is too obvious.

Next door is the master control room. This is an even more complex operation. It looks after the program's pictures. Four people work here. One is a video engineer who monitors the quality of signals coming from the cameras. One is a videotape operator. The third person throws the switches that decide which camera's pictures will be used. The fourth person is David, John Carter's son. He is the director. He tells the cameramen what shots to take and tells the video switcher when to swap cameras.

The worship service starts at 10.45 am and runs for 90 minutes but less than 60 minutes of the program is televised. The service starts with 15 minutes of praise songs led by a singing group. This is not part of the TV program. These songs are followed by a prayer. So far this seems to be a normal worship service. But then it changes.

A man in a suit walks onto the platform and explains the TV production procedures. He asks people to move to the front rows to make it easier for the TV cameras to get crowd shots without seeing empty seats. No-one moves because the congregation members know the routine and have already filled the front seats. However, the announcement lets visitors know what is required if they come again. The man then asks people in the front row to place their purses and books under their seats so the floor doesn't look untidy on camera. He asks people not to pay attention to the cameras when their red lights flick on and off. He asks people to turn off their mobile phones. And he asks people who must leave during the meeting to go out via the back doors—so they don't walk in front of a camera.

The organist and the solo singer remove their wedding rings. Such rings are taboo in some cultures where the program will be viewed.

Cameras roll. John Carter walks onto the stage and says a few words.

He particularly welcomes a new country taking his TV program. He introduces a musical item. And then, everything stops!

A technician rushes to the stage and takes away the speaker's lectern. They don't want it to clutter the stage during the musical item. About a minute after Carter announced the soloist, a voice from an unseen person comes through the church PA system. David, the director, says they are rolling tape again. And a minute after she was announced, the soloist walks onto the stage and sings one item. Her music is quite different to the music 15 minutes earlier. Her song has been chosen to match the music genre normal on 3ABN, more conservative than the music sung before the recording began.

The soloist finishes, walks off stage and everything stops again. The technician returns the lectern to the stage. The unseen voice says the tape is rolling. And 60 seconds after she has left the stage, Carter thanks the soloist for her song and introduces Beverley Carter.

Beverley speaks for five minutes. Then the procedure is repeated for the soloist's second song.

This ritual of removing or replacing the lectern happens five times on this particular day. But strangely enough, rather than being distracting, for those in the congregation it adds to the anticipation.

During the next week, *The Carter Report* technicians will edit the videotape to remove these 60-second gaps. The total editing process will take between 20 and 100 hours. Most viewers won't know the pauses were ever there.

Carter spent Friday away from the office preparing today's sermon. He sent a fax of his sermon notes to his special projects assistant Daniel Burgos, who spent his Friday preparing PowerPoint slides for the sermon. Daniel now sits at a computer booth at the rear of the church with a copy of the sermon notes. He knows what Carter is about to say and at appropriate times he projects the slides onto a giant screen above Carter's head.

The TV cameras do not film the pictures on that large screen. Instead, editors will add them one by one next week.

Ready camera two. . . . Dissolve to two. Ready camera one. . . . Dissolve to one. Get a tight shot camera two. Standby two. Ready to do a slow pull camera two. Dissolve to two. . . . You're doing a great job there camera two.

In the master control room, David Carter's voice is constantly and calmly telling everyone what to do next. As director, the standard of the finished product is almost entirely in his hands. He tells cameras one, two and three what shots he wants next. But only occasionally does he call for a shot from camera four, the camera on the crane.

The main program is a mix of shots taken by cameras one, two and three. They are all taking shots of what is happening on the stage and a mixture of their shots is recorded onto one videotape.

Camera four is taking shots of the audience, and these are recorded onto a separate tape. The best of these audience shots will be added to the main tape next week. This editing takes extra time but it saves the embarrassment of starting to video someone in the audience just as they yawn.

Ready camera three. . . . Dissolve to three. David Carter cannot actually see what is happening in the church. All he sees are four small black-and-white television screens showing what each of the four cameras are filming. He also has two large colour monitors. One shows what is currently being recorded. The other is the preview monitor, showing what is on the camera he plans to use next. In the hour of recording, David calmly calls more than 1000 instructions to his team. There is a lot happening in the master control room.

Standby two. Ready for a slow push, camera two. Carter begins to move.

Stay with him three. And camera three operator pans to the right following Carter as he walks across the stage. *Standby two. . . . Dissolve to camera two.* Each cameraman has a headset to listen to David's instructions. *We're doing good, guys. We're having a good day today.* As well as giving instructions, David is regularly praising his camera crew. *That's good camera three. Well done.*

Toward the end of the hour the tension in the master control room has eased. A few little jokes slip into the director's comments. *It's good to have the A-team here today. Everyone's doing well, except for Jon Palmer.* Jon Palmer is the video engineer sitting in the same room, and he starts laughing along with all the others.

There is an atomic clock in the master control, counting backwards. The clock tells how long they have until the end of the program. David can stop the clock whenever they stop recording. And he can start it again when the program resumes. The time on this clock is also displayed on another clock in the front row of pews for Carter to see. It currently shows they are nearing the end of the program. But when the clock eventually reaches zero, Carter doesn't stop.

"It's always better to have a little too much video, than not enough," David explains with a grin. "We will shorten it when we edit it during the week."

Allowing John to go overtime means Carter doesn't have to stretch or cut short his conclusion. So the ending doesn't lose its punch. The video editors will remove a less-important part of the program to make the show run exactly 58 minutes and 30 seconds.

Slow pull camera three. You are the closing shot.

Set up a slow pull, camera two, as the alternate closing shot.

Then suddenly it's over. The audience was quiet. No mobile phones rang. And no-one walked in front of a camera.

EARLY DAYS IN AUSTRALIA

During the Great Depression of the 1930s, James Carter was one of millions of unemployed men. James looked for work in Brisbane, Australia, but there were no jobs anywhere in his home town. Eventually, he found work out of town, building Somerset Dam, a water-supply reservoir for the city.

James Carter was a Catholic, his wife, Jean, was a Protestant, in an era when Catholics and Protestants were strongly divided. These bitter divisions would split the Carter family for the next half-century.

One serious example of these divisions was when Jean Carter's second child was born. She left her firstborn in the care of the child's grandmother. A few days after the birth, a mob formed at the Catholic church nearby. They wanted to make sure the firstborn child would be a Catholic. So they stormed the house, almost strangled John Carter's grandmother and kidnapped the terrified girl. They planned to take the infant back to the church for the priest to baptise her. But the child's mother found out. Jean jumped out of her hospital bed and caught up with the mob and snatched the infant from them.

The men in the mob were construction workers, each much stronger than this frail woman recovering from childbirth. But her fury was so strong they dared not snatch the child back from her. There was no baptism that day.

About five years later, baby John was born in that same small hospital. However, the tough construction workers still remembered this small woman's fury. None of them dared to take her on again.

When John was born, his mother knew her son was going to be different. While he was still young, she strongly believed he should become an evangelist. She felt God had a special work for her son to do. She didn't tell her child. And she especially didn't tell her Catholic husband. But within her own heart, she dedicated baby John to the work of the ministry, even though she was not an active member of any church.

According to his sister, Margaret, John was a good student at school. He regularly did hours of homework at night without being told to. Margaret describes John as being conscientious, even at a young age. And she says John was a happy child. Even though five years younger than her, John was her best friend.

John developed into a good artist, particularly a landscape artist, winning prizes for art in his teenage years. However, his busy life in ministry meant art largely dropped out of his life.

Even today Carter is missing an eyebrow. This was the result of a fall from an enormous mango tree in his Brisbane backyard. Mango trees are famous for two things: luscious fruit, which in this climate is ripe in late January, and being a good tree for children to climb. John's mother, however, had said he wasn't to climb it.

One day John and his sister—who admits she was a tomboy— shook the mango tree hoping to dislodge some ripe fruit. However, a colony of bees or wasps in the tree didn't take kindly to the shaking. And John and his sister had multiple stings as they ran to the house for shelter.

But the tree wouldn't go away. Every time young John went into the backyard, the tree was still there, tempting him to climb it. One day a metal bucket was left underneath the tree. A six-year-old boy wouldn't even notice that bucket while climbing into the greenery. But John fell from the tree, his face hitting the bucket's sharp edge, slicing off his eyebrow.

Just beyond the mango tree was the south bank of the Brisbane River. At this point the river is about 400 metres (a quarter of a mile) wide. John lived the carefree days of his young life in this idyllic location at the river's edge. The family of five lived on two large building blocks, which had an old weatherboard house with two verandas—"a Queenslander," the traditional style of home in Queensland. The house was built up in the air so breezes could circulate underneath and cool it down. The home was located about eight kilometres (five miles) from the centre of the city of Brisbane, and Carter's earliest memories are of this house.

The kitchen was always half-full of smoke from the wood stove that cooked the family meals. Young John's eyes burned when he went into the kitchen. In the outside wall was a big glass sliding window with a heavy wooden frame. "We had it open a lot of the time to let the smoke escape," he recalls. "The window acted like a chimney."

While living there, John had several serious bouts of illness. He had rheumatic fever, which created a heart murmur he still has. And he developed double pneumonia and was taken out of school for 12 months to recover.

John had a bed on one of the wide verandas so he would get fresh air for his recovery. In late spring and in summer, Brisbane evenings are often treated to wild electrical storms. Carter still remembers how much he liked to watch those fireworks displays. He was not one of those who feared the storms. He loved them.

John spent much of his time outdoors. His mother helped him build a raft to enjoy the days of his recuperation. Together they attached a rope to the raft and secured the other end to a tree on the shore. Then Jean launched her son into the water at the end of the rope to pretend he was Huckleberry Finn or a pirate—or whatever his imagination wanted him to be.

John did a lot of fishing from that raft. "I would catch fish, prawns and crabs," says Carter. "I don't eat any of those things now, but I ate them all then. I remember catching a mud crab in a net. My mother was looking out the window. The crab was so big when it reared up on its hind legs and put out its big pincers that my mother said, 'I wonder, who caught who?'"

The owner of the house also lived there. He let the struggling Carter family live there rent free. In return, Jean Carter prepared his meals. When the owner eventually wanted to sell the house, he offered it to the Carters, allowing them to pay it off weekly with no interest. "My father had come out of the Great Depression and was too afraid," Carter explains. "He said it was too much of a risk. That huge double block would be worth $5 million now. That's when I missed out on becoming a millionaire," Carter reminisces with a laugh.

Next door to this big house lived a woman called Mrs Scott. Carter cannot remember her first name. He used to call her Mrs Dot, although Dot wasn't her name. Young John simply called her that because he couldn't properly pronounce the word *Scott*. It is a surprising fact that John, now a renowned public speaker, spoke very poorly as a child. His poor speaking ability was a major impediment. Even at seven years of age, he could not say "Scott."

"Some of my happiest memories were visiting Mrs Scott's home as a boy. She would feed me mouldy chocolate. It always looked like it had been there for years.

"Once she caused a bit of consternation for my mother. She had a canoe. With me in it she rowed right across the river at its widest point, navigating all the shipping. She didn't tell my mother. But my mother could see it all from her kitchen window and didn't think we would survive.

"Years later, Mrs Scott came to my graduation at Avondale College. She had travelled 600 miles [1000 kilometres] to see it. Everybody loved Mrs Scott."

A SPIRITUAL JOURNEY BEGINS

Young John's spiritual pilgrimage began in Queensland when he was seven years old. In 1946, American evangelist Clifford Reeves held an evangelistic series in Brisbane's City Hall. John's mother went to hear him and liked what she heard, so she kept attending his meetings for about six months. She was convicted, converted and baptised.

Jean was excited by what she discovered in the Bible and wanted to share it. She would stand on her veranda giving Bible studies to Mrs Scott next door, who in turn was standing on her veranda. Young John was amused to watch this. "To me it was like two battleships with sailors on the decks. My mother was leaning over her parapet and Mrs Scott was leaning over hers."

But as well as entertaining the growing boy, these discussions also had an impact on Mrs Scott, who in due course was also baptised as an Adventist Christian.

One day, not long before they moved out of the house on the river, Jean glanced out the kitchen window toward a nearby shipyard. She saw a group of black men with fuzzy hair. Jean told her son to get his blackboard and on it she wrote "7 day." She held it up and when the men saw it, they ran up to her house. They too were Seventh-day Adventists. In fact, they were not just ordinary Seventh-day Adventists. They were some of the legendary "Fuzzy Wuzzy Angels" who helped win the Second World War by their bravery on the infamous Kokoda Track in Papua New Guinea.

Now, just a year after the war ended, John has a half-dozen of these legendary Fuzzy Wuzzy Angels running up toward his house. "They came and talked and sang in our home each night for two weeks—fabulous harmony," he remembers. "It touched my heart tremendously. What a boost to our faith just after we had become Adventists."

These "angels" were there because they had sailed an Adventist mission boat to Brisbane for repairs. After two weeks, they sailed home, but left an indelible impression on the seven-year-old boy. Years later he would visit their homeland and lead hundreds to Christ.

John's boyhood home on the river led the family to meet another Adventist legend. Her name was Alma Wiles. When she was newly married in 1914, she and her husband, Norman, had gone to the New Hebrides (now Vanuatu) as missionaries.

"They were all alone on a mission station many miles from civilisation," Carter recalls. "The natives there were still savages and cannibals. Norman died of blackwater fever, the first Adventist missionary to die in the South Pacific. Alma dug his grave and buried him. Then she sat guard on the grave for days so the natives wouldn't dig him up and eat him. She sent a messenger to report what happened. They came and got her and she was taken back to Australia. And after a period of mourning, she went back as a missionary."

Word reached John's mother that Alma was on a ship they could see docked on the other side of the river. "I remember my mother taking me on board to meet her," says Carter. "My mother wanted to talk to her because she was having marriage problems as a result of becoming a Seventh-day Adventist. Mrs Wiles put me on her knee and encouraged me. 'Maybe God wants you to become a missionary one day,' she said. That's an impression I have never forgotten."

Ten years after John was encouraged to become a missionary, he enrolled at Australasian Missionary College, which changed its name to Avondale College in 1964. One of the first things he saw on the campus was a memorial to Norman Wiles, the first missionary from the college to die on duty. It brought back memories of Norman's wife who had sat at that graveside and who had sat young John on her knee.

When she was newly baptised, Jean Carter started attending the Adventist church in the Brisbane suburb of Morningside. She took an unwilling seven-year-old John with her. His father was bitterly opposed. He resisted every religious step his family took. It would be another 40 years before his father was also baptised. But Jean eventually saw her husband, her two daughters and her two sons baptised as Adventist Christians.

John's first regular encounter with the Bible was at Morningside Sabbath school. His teacher was impressed by young John. He felt the boy was very spiritual and enthusiastic and could achieve a lot for God. John himself didn't see that, and within a few years his life took a different direction.

When John was a young teenager, he felt very lost and lonely. He felt a great need, but didn't know what it was. He did things that today seem mild, but were "pretty wild" for a Christian young person of his day. John had an irresistible conviction he would become a minister. His lifestyle, however, did not match his intentions.

One night he and a few rebellious friends decided they would go to a spiritualist meeting. They changed their mind, but John dwelled on the ideas of satanism. That night he went home and locked the back door as usual. There had been a prowler in the area, so his father had put a large padlock on the door as an extra lock.

Two or three times during the night John's father woke up because there was a wind blowing through the house. He got up and locked both the back door lock and the padlock. An hour or so later the wind blew through the house again. His father went to the back door and found the door unlocked again. Several times he locked the door during the night—and each time it unlocked itself.

At the breakfast table next morning, his father told how the door kept unlocking. "It's almost as if we had a sympathiser of spiritualism in the house," his mother said.

"I was so scared that I told my mother exactly where I had wanted to go the night before," Carter recalls. "She said, 'Well, the devil's after you.'"

The shock helped turn him around.

A pastor who knew John well was astonished that this young "rebel" wanted to train as a minister. "I'd be surprised if that boy wasn't expelled," he commented.

MAKING AN EVANGELIST

John Carter studied for his degree at Avondale College, the university-level college that trains Australia's Adventist ministers. This was the most astounding spiritual experience of his life. "I found Jesus, my Lord and Saviour, at Avondale," he says.

Avondale College was the greatest turning point in his life. There he saw the truths of the gospel in sharper focus. He would never lose the joy of salvation he discovered at Avondale.

"I went to Avondale as a needy young person," Carter says. "I was immediately impressed by the wonderful spirit there."

Carter was befriended by Tom Ludowici, a ministerial student who had a burden to help younger students find the Lord. After the meetings of the college's Week of Prayer, Tom took John and a few others out under the trees at night. There Tom taught him to pray.

"When I gave my life to Christ I felt that I owned Him and He owned me," says Carter. "I was dumbfounded by His love. And it is true, even though it is a cliché, that the sky was bluer and the birds sung sweeter. It was the most wonderful experience of my life. I felt so uplifted and so blessed."

Young men who train as ministers can follow many different paths. They can become pastors, church administrators, youth leaders or fill a dozen other niches. For Carter there was only one option—an evangelist.

The Avondale College motto was, "For a greater vision of world needs." The motto was on the badge Carter pinned to his jacket. It was engraved in stone outside some of the college dormitories and on the wall of the chapel where Carter and the other students regularly worshipped. Carter caught the vision. His parish would not just be a small corner of the globe. His parish would be the world. (The statement "My parish is the world" was first made by John Wesley, the founder of what became the Methodist Church.)

John Carter was at Avondale for two years before he began his four-year theology degree. At the beginning of his fourth year at college, he noticed a new student named Beverley Buchanan. "She seemed special from the first time I saw her," says John. What impressed him about Beverley was that "she was earnest and sincere."

Beverley was taking the Bible instructors course. That was in the years before women could become church pastors, so women who felt such a calling studied this course and, when they graduated, assisted in running evangelistic campaigns.

The Adventist Church had a scholarship scheme to help young people who could not pay their Avondale College fees. The young people could sell religious books door-to-door to earn part of their fees, then the church scholarship fund would pay the rest of their fees.

John and Beverley spent several summer vacations selling books together. Beverley stayed at John's parents' home in Brisbane. They didn't have a car, or even enough money to pay for a bus or a tram fare. So each morning they walked eight kilometres to the area in which they planned to sell. Then each evening they would walk home. Daily walking became a permanent part of both their lives.

Carter describes this door-to-door work as "trying to sell books to people who didn't want them." Church administrators considered this was good training for the ministry—where pastors often try to present the gospel to people who don't want it. But Beverley was a much better salesperson than John. She had the best sales figures for the whole of Australia.

John had not completed high school when he enrolled at Avondale. So before he began the ministerial course, he had to complete his high school diploma. In the first three years of his ministerial course he was only an average student. But he planned to marry Beverley at the end of his final year and in that year he went from an average pupil to a straight "A" student. He leapt to the top of the class.

A few months after Carter graduated, the couple married. And a few days after that they were on a 1000-kilometre (600-mile) train journey to one of the most isolated cities in the world. At Broken Hill—deep in Australia's outback—Carter served his apprenticeship as an assistant pastor and evangelist.

For the next 20 years, the Carters and their growing family moved house almost every year. In city after city in the eastern states of Australia, Carter held evangelistic campaigns, generally lasting about nine months. He would hold two public meetings each week in the city's biggest public hall. For the rest of the week, he would visit the homes of people attending his program and give them personal Bible studies. Before any of these people were baptised, they studied the Bible for 50-100 hours.

Carter's success in the smaller cities meant every transfer was to a larger city. Eventually he was transferred to the two biggest cities in the country: Melbourne, Victoria, in 1979, followed by Sydney, New South Wales, in 1982.

Because fewer than 10 per cent of Australians are regular churchgoers, advertising that evangelists used to attract an audience in the United States did not work in Australia. Because relatively few Australians attend religious programs, Australian evangelists developed a different approach—archaeology.

For a decade before John Carter cut his teeth in the tough world of evangelism, Australian evangelists had used archaeology to lure a crowd. Thousands came to Adventist programs held in the smallest hamlets to the largest cities. And in these archaeology meetings, the evangelists explained how the discoveries of archaeology verified that the Bible is correct. Once they established that Scripture could be trusted, the programs would begin to explain what the Bible actually teaches.

Significantly, this extra introductory step in Australian evangelistic campaigns became a major key for success when the USSR started to shed Communism and open up for the Christian message.

The Australian evangelists—more used to speaking to audiences who did not have a background in Christianity—had the advantage.

In Australia, Carter hadn't created the concept of using archaeology as the basis for an evangelistic campaign. He inherited the concepts of successfully using low budgets and archaeology from the Australian evangelists who went before him. But he did lift this method of evangelism to a new level of success.

One of Carter's innovations was his use of TV. An Adventist friend was the producer a five-minute secular program on commercial TV. Carter liked the program and wanted to adapt it to make a religious version of the show. At the time, he was planning an evangelistic series at Albury-Wodonga, the largest city on the 1000-kilometre (600-mile) Victoria–New South Wales border. He arranged for his friend to write the script.

Carter wanted to call it *Amazing Discoveries,* a name he had always used. His friend wanted to call it *The Carter Report,* which John thought seemed egotistical. "What would the other evangelists think of me?" he argued.

"I don't care what the other evangelists think," the producer replied. "I'm after results and this name will give us better results." Carter has used that name for his TV programs and website ever since.

The Carter Report ran at 8.30 most weeknights for several weeks. Carter was the on-camera host. It was one of the few religious programs anywhere in the world good enough for a secular TV station to show in a peak timeslot. While Carter paid for the timeslot, the station wouldn't have let it go to air if it were below standard. It astonished staff at the station to see religious programs as good as peak-viewing secular programs. The segments were mainly on archaeology, showing how its discoveries verify the Bible. The message was similar to what he later gave in the first week of his evangelistic programs in Russia.

Carter was a television natural. He had trained as a public speaker at Avondale College, and he did a good job of adapting that training to TV. He so impressed the managers of the Albury station, they offered him a job as a newsreader.

He returned to TV advertising in the lead-up to his evangelistic series in Melbourne, Australia's second largest city, again breaking new ground.

TV had become the enemy of evangelism in Australia. People

wanted to stay home and watch TV instead of going out on a cold night to hear about the Bible and archaeology. It had been 20 years since the Adventist Church's last successful capital city evangelistic campaign in Australia. Then Pastor John Coltheart—who created the concept of using archaeology for evangelism—had 5000 people come to the opening night of his "Dead men do tell tales" program.

The advertising for the Melbourne program was simple. Carter and a TV film crew travelled to Egypt. There he stood in front of ancient monuments and talked to viewers about his forthcoming meetings. The scripts followed this basic pattern:

I'm John Carter and this is the bearded queen, mystery woman of ancient Egypt. Who was she? Did she really have a beard? Why did pharaoh disfigure her face and why is her mummy the only one missing? I'll answer these questions and more at Dallas Brooks Hall this weekend.

A phone number was superimposed on the bottom of the screen while John Carter talked. And in the last 10 seconds of the 30-second advertisement, an off-camera announcer told viewers how to book seats for the meeting. So many people dialled the advertised phone number the local telephone exchange burnt out.

The local telephone company phoned the Carter office. They reported that whenever the advertisements went to air, the resulting calls short-circuited half the phone lines through the exchange. Thousands of callers were being constantly disconnected. Despite these difficulties, the program opened with five identical sessions on its first weekend, with attendance totalling 12,500.

A significant innovation introduced in Carter's Melbourne program was a fundraising newsletter. Normally, Adventist evangelists don't develop fundraising skills because church administration provides finance for their meetings. The cost of

Carter's program was to be paid equally by three levels of church administration. However, the regular election of officers appointed a new president and committee for the local conference. The new committee planned to discontinue their support of the series for financial reasons.

After some negotiations, the committee backed down from cancelling the program but left Carter to raise the necessary funds. Having to raise the money seemed like a huge setback. However, Carter didn't complain. He just got on with the extra job they had given him to do.

Carter had a friend who owned Australia's largest newsletter publishing company. His friend helped by writing regular fundraising newsletters to be distributed to church members. Carter's fundraising was so successful it raised four times more money than needed.

The first of these *Carter Report* newsletters explained the new evangelism advertising that would be used in Melbourne. "If we succeed here," the newsletter said, "this concept can be used for evangelism in major cities worldwide."

Despite the challenge this posed at the time, this strategy had two advantages. First, when members contributed financially, it made them more enthusiastic to support the project personally. Second, Carter learned the skills of fundraising and of producing fundraising newsletters. These abilities would become very important for financing evangelism in Russia.

After his successful campaign in Melbourne, Carter was asked to run a program in Sydney. This time the finance was assured and the venue was instantly recognisable: the Sydney Opera House on the shore of Sydney Harbour.

In 1982, *The Carter Report* attracted an audience of 18,000 people, the largest attendance ever seen inside the venerable concert halls. The venue itself seated only 3000 people but Carter held six identical meetings on the one weekend so no-one would be turned away. And again so many people called the phone number given in TV advertising that it burnt out the local telephone exchange.

Pastors from all 50 Adventist churches in Sydney were part of *The Carter Report* team. The nine-month program was highly successful and another program was planned for the following year. But most of the church pastors said they couldn't spend two consecutive years doing reduced duties as local church ministers.

Years earlier, at a Carter team meeting in a small country town, someone suggested the team train church members to give Bible studies to people who attended. "I wouldn't give one of my contacts to a layperson to follow up," Carter responded emphatically.

Fourteen years later, he had no choice. He had a major campaign coming up in Australia's largest city, but he had few pastors to take the follow-up Bible studies. He had no choice but to bring local church members into his team—and it worked well.

From that time on, Carter duplicated that concept wherever he held an evangelistic series. In his first major series in Russia, for example, he had only a handful of ministers on his team. But he also had 50 church members—and that program resulted in 2500 baptisms.

It seems God was training Carter for the tasks that lay ahead.

PRAYING BEHIND THE CURTAIN

Beverley Carter was raised as the eldest daughter on a small farm, 30 kilometres (18 miles) from the nearest town. Her family did not attend church but her parents taught her to work hard, always be honest and to respect everyone.

When she was 16, her boyfriend (coincidentally named John) was killed in a car accident involving a drunk driver. Beverley was the last person to see him alive.

"That led me to read the Bible to study about death. I didn't know it, but my mother had bought the two volumes of *The Desire of Ages*. I found them, and especially read the chapter on the Resurrection. That gave me great encouragement and led me to read the Bible more."

Beverley knew she could have been in the car with her boyfriend that night. She thanked God she wasn't killed, probably the first prayer of a woman now known around the world for her prayer life.

After the accident, the spectre of death haunted her. "I had a vision of the whole world rushing toward death. I needed to get right with God. I needed to do something with my life to help others. The burden came on me to tell others to get ready for death."

"I prayed, 'God, what church do you want me to join?'" She visited all the churches in Goomeri, the nearest town to her family's farm, but none of them satisfied her.

"I continued to study the Bible, but I hadn't found a church. One day I was reading the Ten Commandments. The fourth commandment leaped out at me. *The seventh day is the Sabbath.* I asked myself, 'Why does everyone go to church on Sunday, the first day of the week? Is there a church that goes to church on Saturday?'"

She asked her friends if there was such a church. She found out there was one, but it was 110 kilometres (66 miles) away in the Queensland country town of Kingaroy.

"Providentially, my best girlfriend's mother was being visited by the Seventh-day Adventist pastor from Kingaroy. I told my friend, 'Let me know the next time he comes because I want to be there. I have some questions to ask him.'"

The next time Pastor Edwin Gallagher completed his circuit, young Beverley was there to meet him.

"The first question I asked him," she recalls, "was 'Who changed the Sabbath from Saturday to Sunday?' He gave me a Bible study from Daniel 7 showing how the day was changed. I didn't know anything about church history and was surprised to find out. But it was marvellous to discover that it was predicted in the Bible. From then on, when the pastor came once a month, I was there to have my own Bible study with him."

Beverley decided she wanted to go to the church that met on Saturdays. Every second Friday, she travelled into town and caught the one train a day that went to Kingaroy.

"I stayed in the Gallagher family's home. They treated me like their own daughter. I thank God Pastor Gallagher was a true gospel preacher. The gospel I heard from him was not legalistic."

But Beverley's parents were very much against what their 17-year-old daughter was doing.

Her father was a heavy drinker. During World War II, he had been sent to the Kokoda Track when he was only 20. He started drinking a lot because of the pressures of battle. And he kept drinking afterwards to forget the horrors of war.

"My father went away for a week on a binge. We didn't know where he was. A neighbour said to me, 'It's your fault. He's worried that you're joining a cult.'

"Then I felt that a heavy weight, a blackness, was holding me. A voice said, 'Look what this religion is doing. It is tearing your family apart.' But another voice said, 'If you don't do this, you won't be saved and you'll never have the opportunity to help your family spiritually.' This battle of voices continued for several minutes.

"I realised I had to make a decision then. I know the Lord was helping me. I had to do what was right. So I decided. And once I had made that decision, the blackness lifted.

"After it lifted, I shook for several minutes. I guess it was a reaction to the battle in my mind—or the battle *for* my mind. My mother took hold of my shaking hands and gave me a cup of tea"—which was a typical Australian bush way of solving any problem.

Shortly afterwards, Beverley was baptised at Kingaroy Adventist church. It was in November 1958, almost exactly 12 months since her boyfriend had been killed.

The following year, a number of young people from Kingaroy

church went to Avondale College. They suggested Beverley come with them.

"My family didn't want me to go, but I prayed that the Lord would touch my dad's heart. The Lord worked a miracle because, even though he didn't want me to go to Avondale, he gave me some money for my first year.

"My plan was to spend a year there, then go to the Sydney Adventist Hospital to do nursing. I wanted to become a missionary nurse to Africa. That was my dream. I even wrote to Dr Albert Schweitzer and got a nice letter back from his secretary saying missionary nurses were very much needed."

At this time, John Carter was helping to pay for his fees by operating the checkout at the college cafeteria. Doing this task he quickly knew every student living in the college. While John noticed Beverley straightaway, it took a while for Beverley to realise John existed.

"He asked me out for a date. It was probably a games evening at the college auditorium. We enjoyed each other's company and we kept going out on dates. The thing that drew us together was that we both had the same dream of giving our lives in service to God."

Beverley changed her mind about becoming a nurse and enrolled in the Bible Instructor's Course. "This was the best decision I could have made. It certainly helped me in my work as a minister's wife."

Three years after the couple met, they were married on March 4, 1962. John took up his duties as assistant pastor and evangelist in outback Broken Hill. Beverley worked for the first year of their marriage selling religious books door-to-door in that town.

"I wore out three pairs of shoes, but I earned enough money to buy our first car—a little blue Volkswagen."

In the early days of John's ministry, Beverley was effectively his assistant pastor. "In our age, all of the ministers' wives supported their husbands. There wasn't enough money for the conference to provide an assistant minister, so the wife was the assistant.

"I would be the head usherette at an evangelistic program. I would train church members how to welcome the people as they arrived. I arranged the giving out of the Bibles. And I taught the church members how to look after people and how to help the people at the meetings.

"Both John and I love evangelism. Both of us have a burden to see people saved."

"She believes that if a church doesn't evangelise, it will die," Carter says of his wife. "That's a core belief for her."

In the Russian programs, Beverley runs the morning team devotional period each day. These are designed to bring team members closer to God and to help them bond with each other.

Beverley usually takes a five-minute talk when Carter's church services are televised. Her talks are on spiritual themes and are quite different from what her husband says.

She reads several books a month, usually devotional books and biographies. She also reads magazines on current issues, especially articles about young people and children. Beverley is also interested in the world's environmental problems.

From the day she was converted, prayer has always been an important part of her life. Whenever her husband wanted to attempt something big for God, and everyone said it couldn't be done, Beverley would pray for success.

However, her famous "praying behind the curtain" didn't begin until she and her husband had worked in ministry for 30 years. She had always prayed for God's blessing on Carter *before* his evangelistic meetings. But when she and John first arrived in Russia, she felt an even greater need for prayer.

"There was a bigger battle there," she says, "because the devil had had his way with that nation for 70 years."

Beverley began standing behind the curtain on the stage, praying while her husband was preaching. If Carter is preaching for an hour, Beverley prays for that hour. Sometimes she stands still. Sometimes she walks back and forth behind the curtain. Sometimes she sits. But always she is praying.

She prays for practical things. Russia was renowned for its blackouts. But during each of her husband's meetings, Beverley prayed for God to protect the power supply. And there has never been a blackout at a Carter meeting in Russia or Ukraine.

Beverley's prayers are also tied in to what her husband is saying. "I know how a non-Christian is going to react. So I'm thinking what their reaction will be, and I am praying about that reaction. I'm not just saying, 'God bless John; God bless the people. God bless John; God bless the people.'

"I'm listening to what John is saying and I'm praying about that. I pray for John and for the translator. I pray for the sound equipment. I pray for the lighting. I pray that people not used to sitting still can sit still.

"I pray, 'Please God, make it so the people can understand that point. Please make the evangelist clear.'

"By the end of the session, I'm exhausted. I have fatigue because I've been concentrating so much."

Beverley is the prayer coordinator for her local church. She heads a group of 15 praying people in that church. Prayer requests come to her and she emails them to the prayer group. On Sabbaths, she prays for the worship service, and especially for the TV crew on the days the service will be televised.

However, her prayer ministry goes much further than just her local church. Her prayer ministry goes worldwide through the <cartereport.org> website.

"I believe prayer is more than 'saying prayers,'" she reflects. "It is built on a relationship with our heavenly Father and prayer is our conversation with Him.

"After learning the doctrines of the Bible, the most important thing is to read the Bible with prayer to see how God wants me to live day by day. For me, being an authentic Christian is living, or obeying, God's will for my life. The only way I can find out what that is, is by reading the Bible."

Beverley cares for her health with a strong exercise program. She went to the gym at 5.30 every morning for many years. Now she's reached retirement age, she still walks every day for 30-60 minutes, usually on a treadmill.

Health is important to Beverley. She realises it's taxing work being an evangelist. "John is one of the few Anglos who has stayed an evangelist until retirement," she says.

Ask her what has kept Carter healthy so long and she replies in a confident tone, "I'm the cook!"

CARTER'S ASTONISHING ADVERTISING

Executives from the worldwide *Reader's Digest* organisation are astonished by what they have seen. They want to have the best advertising writers in the world to promote the *Reader's Digest*. But now they have seen advertising that astounds them. They want to have advertising this good for themselves.

John Carter's phone rings. "Your advertising is the slickest we have seen anywhere in the world," a *Reader's Digest* executive tells him. "Could you tell us who your advertising agency is?"

But Carter has no advertising agency. His ads were created by himself and some of his Seventh-day Adventist friends.

His advertising has four key elements: television, brochures, outdoor advertising and radio. He also used newspaper advertising until his last few campaigns in the former USSR.

Carter doesn't usually seek free media publicity until after his program has started. This prevents a cynical or anti-Christian journalist undermining the program before it starts. If he had to have only two forms of advertising, he says they would be television and brochures.

Brochures

Carter's advertising brochure works incredibly well. He hasn't found any reason to significantly change it since it was designed 25 years ago. It was created at Signs Publishing Company by a graphic artist named Alan Holman.

It is a quality brochure with four colours and four pages. The front page is black and gold, and it features a large photo of Pharaoh Tutankhamen's death mask. It has a *Carter Report* logo, and the words "Amazing Discoveries in Lost Cities of the Dead. Shrine Auditorium."

The double page inside gives details of the first five programs.

The back page of the brochure has photographs of the venue and of Carter. The caption for Carter's photo on the back page says: "John Carter is an Australian who specialises in the great themes of the Bible. He takes his audience on a remarkable journey in the footsteps of the prophets, through the heyday of forgotten empires. His lectures on four continents have generated tremendous interest and enthusiasm. Millions say, 'These are the greatest meetings I have ever attended. I would not have missed them for anything.'"

Carter's brochures are delivered to every mailbox in a Russian city. Plus teams of Adventists give them out at the top of the stairs as people leave the underground railway. And each church member is given a few to use when inviting friends to the meetings.

Television

Carter usually has about five different TV scripts to promote his opening program. The first 20 seconds of those 30-second ads feature John on camera. Here are a few of those scripts:

Carter on location outside King Tut's tomb in Egypt: "I'm John Carter in Egypt to check the most sensational archaeological discovery in 100 years. What did they find in the fabulous tomb of Tutankhamen? Did Pharaoh place a curse on those who opened this tomb? Can that curse still kill today? I'll answer these questions and more at Kiev Palace of Sport this weekend."

Carter on location at Luxor in Egypt: "I'm John Carter in Egypt to investigate the greatest sun temple the world has ever seen. How were these thousand-ton beams lifted 70 feet [21 metres] in the air? How long did this temple take to build? And what amazing message for us today is found in this mysterious writing? I'll answer these questions and more at Sydney Opera House this weekend."

Carter on location at Egypt's great pyramids: "I'm John Carter in the Sahara Desert, investigating secrets of Egypt's greatest pyramid. Who built it? What was hidden in its secret tunnels? And does this pyramid possess secret powers? I'll answer these questions and more at Shrine Auditorium this weekend."

Carter on location at Petra in Jordan: "I'm John Carter in Petra, the city carved from a red-rock mountain. What strange religious rites were practised here? Why was Petra lost for 1000 years? And why did Bible prophets predict its destruction? I'll answer these questions and more at Gorky Palace of Sport this weekend."

The last 10 seconds of the advertisement gives the times and days of the meeting.

Carter's TV advertisements ask a series of questions. He makes sure to answer each of those questions clearly in the opening program. Each question takes about five seconds to answer, so answering them all is not a large part of the program. But answering them is essential to avoid audience dissatisfaction.

Outdoor

In Russia, the law allows John to have banners that stretch above busy roads. There are not a lot of words on them: "The Carter Report presents Amazing Discoveries, [time, date and place]."

"Since the Communist Revolution, Russians have been into posters, big posters," says Carter. "So each time that we run a program in a big city in Russia, we put out thousands of posters around the city. The posters are 18 inches [half a metre] high and have a picture of King Tut's death mask. Printed below it are the details of the meeting."

Russian cities have a lot of bus, train and tram services, so Carter pays to have these posters on and in every one of them. Plus he pays a professional firm to paste the posters in prominent places in the city.

In every big campaign in Russia, Carter has about six large billboards in the centre of the city. He says he would do this in the West only if it were economical.

Radio

Carter's radio advertisements are quite different from the TV ads. They create an image of mystery. Carter wrote and reads the radio scripts himself:

"Don't miss Amazing Discoveries in Lost Cities of the Dead. This Saturday. Sydney Opera House. Exploring mysterious cities . . . deserted palaces . . . and fabulous temples, in the mystical lands of the Middle East. Proof of God from the land of the Pharaohs.

Millions around the world say, this is the greatest program I've ever seen. Be there when John Carter reveals 'I saw divine predictions fulfilled.' For your free tickets, call now. Phone 9876 5432. Bookings are flooding in. Avoid disappointment. Call now. Phone 9876 5432. Don't let your best friend or your worst enemy cause you to miss this astounding presentation. This Saturday. Sydney Opera House at 3 and 7. Be there."

✳ ✳ ✳

According to John Carter, the most astonishing thing about his advertising isn't that it is so effective or that successful advertisers like *Reader's Digest* sing its praises. The most astonishing thing about Carter's advertising is that other Adventists across the world don't copy it.

Carter is surprised other pastors don't duplicate these successful brochures to promote their own campaigns. And he is astounded more evangelists don't fly to Egypt with a TV crew and video these advertisements.

A CURE FOR YOUTH PROBLEMS

The Seventh-day Adventist Church owns the highest block of land in Australia's biggest city. On this large site overlooking Sydney is the headquarters of the church in the South Pacific Division. At the peak of the hill is the renowned Sydney Adventist Hospital. Also in this cluster of buildings you will find an Adventist TV studio, plus the largest Adventist church in Australia.

John Carter played a role at all of these buildings. He was on the South Pacific Division executive committee. He worked closely with the TV studio as a pioneer of the concept of making Christian videos. He made pastoral visits to patients in the hospital. And in 1984, he was made the pastor of this large church.

Carter loved the job as the Wahroonga church pastor. He considered the congregation one of the finest in the world—but one thing troubled him. A group of young people seemed to have lost their connection with the gospel, becoming legalistic and critical. Carter tried friendship, Bible study and discussion to cure this religious illness. He even wrote a booklet for them called *The Big Issues of the Gospel*, explaining that we are saved by faith not works.

But nothing seemed to work.

As the pastor and his wife discussed what to do about it, Beverley came up with a suggestion: distract the young people from their theological wrangling. Take them away from the negative environment they are locked into. Get them to do something practical, involving them in real Christian witnessing in a developing nation.

About 6000 kilometres (3700 miles) to the north-west lay the 7000 islands that make up the republic of the Philippines. Because it is an English-speaking country close to Australia, this former American colony was a good choice for Beverley's project.

Only a few weeks after the suggestion was made, Carter found himself on a plane to the capital city, Manila. There he booked the 5000-seat Philippine International Convention Center—even though he didn't have the money. He then flew home to Australia to raise the cash and to enthuse young people to join the great adventure. Each young person had to raise the money for their own airfares and accommodation. About 80 of them did so and joined the team.

Carter's archaeology-based advertising electrified Manila. The convention centre was filled six times on the opening weekend, a total attendance of about 30,000 people, with thousands more turned away. The opening featured prominently on local TV news.

During the week, the meeting slipped back to the maximum seating capacity of 5000 each night. Carter hadn't yet struck on the idea of holding weeknight meetings at both 5 pm and 7 pm. That idea came from a Russian church member a few years later. But an unexpected crisis meant that here in Manila he had to borrow that idea from the future. The crisis came after a guest appearance on a breakfast TV chat show.

After a late night from preaching, Carter rose early and was driven to a capital city TV studio. While on air, the show's host said to him, "Your program tonight is about the antichrist. Who is the antichrist?" Carter has a policy to not publicly criticise any organisation, so he feels that he cannot make any suggestions on air about who the antichrist might be.

"I know who the antichrist is, but I feel I cannot tell you," says Carter. "However, in tonight's program I will give the Bible's identifying marks so people can work it out for themselves."

The TV hosts are impressed. They say they both will attend tonight's meeting at the convention centre to discover the answer. Then they recommend that people in the TV audience join them at the Carter program.

Members of the Carter team hope the interview may bring a few extra people to the meeting. But no-one guesses the overwhelming impact it will have.

In the early evening, Carter travels by car to the convention centre. He has plenty of time before the meeting starts. But he is astounded. Streets around the centre are blocked. Traffic is at a standstill. Not only are the roadways totally snarled with cars, the plaza and the footpaths around the centre are crammed with pedestrians. Because this is such a strong Catholic country, people feel a strong need to identify the antichrist. It has brought them out in their thousands.

Armed guards escort Carter through the crowds to the back entrance. Inside, the centre is packed with wall-to-wall people. However, there seem to be more people outside than inside.

Police are concerned the crowd who can't get in might start a riot. The doors have been closed because there is no more room inside. But the police think the force of the mob could break through the front doors. A senior police officer asks him to come outside and speak to the people who cannot get in.

Carter has never had to quell a potential riot. Police hand him a megaphone and he stands on a raised area so people can see him. He raises his hand and lowers it slowly as a gesture for silence. He asks the crowd to be calm. The people become especially quiet when they see that it's Carter himself.

He apologises for the situation. Then he promises he will hold another session of his program as soon as this meeting ends. If they wait for an hour-and-a-half, they can come inside as soon as the others come out.

This reduces the tension outside. Light rain is falling but the people tolerate that once they know there will be a second meeting.

Armed guards stand in prominent places inside the hall, as they do for every meeting. But there are extra guards tonight; soldiers carrying submachine guns have joined Carter's own security staff. It is a particularly tense time, and the soldiers are there to help maintain control. They watch over an audience made up of all classes of society, something Philippine church leaders have never seen at an evangelistic series before. There are bishops, generals, diplomats, politicians, business leaders, priests and nuns, as well as thousands of everyday people. Local church leaders say this is a breakthrough. It's the first time a Protestant campaign has reached the upper classes.

Tonight's meeting is so tense the authorities have security guards at the doors checking people for weapons. (This was in the days when such screening wasn't even done at airports.)

John comments to Beverley, "I might be shot tonight." He's not trying to be melodramatic. He senses there are powers that might not want him to deliver tonight's message. After saying a prayer together, he strides toward the stage. Despite the danger, he believes God has removed all fear from his mind. He walks onto the stage at peace.

The crowd is absolutely silent. Carter asks for a vote. He says that many people do not want him to take tonight's meeting identifying the antichrist. "I want a show of hands," he says. "Should I be completely honest, preach the truth, and hold back nothing? I want to see the hands of those in favour." It seems like every hand is raised in the vast auditorium. "Those against?" Not a single hand rises to suggest he should drop the subject. So he opens his Bible to find identifying marks of the antichrist. He doesn't name any individual or any organisation as being the antichrist but point by point he gives the crowd clues to work it out for themselves.

There is spontaneous applause when Carter finishes. The audience rises and gives him a standing ovation, lasting for several minutes. It is the longest applause John will receive in his entire life. Bishops and priests are among those clapping the hardest. Then when this stunned audience leaves the auditorium, another slightly wet audience comes in to have the same experience.

The son of the nation's president is among the array of dignitaries in the meeting each night. President Ferdinand Marcos has given his son a special assignment. He asks his son to meet the evangelist, which he does between the two meetings. He tells Carter the president is strongly interested in the identity of the antichrist. However, he has a rash on his face and is too embarrassed to be seen in public.

"Before I left the presidential palace tonight," the son tells Carter, "my father suggested that the antichrist might be the Catholic Church." However, the son has now learned that the evangelist hasn't named anyone. Yet President Marcos will not be disappointed in the report his son gives him. He now brings home 15 clear identifying marks from the Bible so the president can find out for himself who the antichrist is.

The local church arranges for Carter to personally give tapes of his meetings to the president. However, the president becomes ill and the visit is cancelled. Yet he does talk personally to the president's wife, Imelda Marcos.

∗ ∗ ∗

A man in Manila plans to commit murder. He conceals a knife in his clothing and goes to where he knows he will find the man he wants to kill. He follows him all day through this city of 10 million people, waiting for a chance to strike. But no opportunity presents itself. In the early evening his victim walks toward the International Convention Center. The victim is going to attend *The Carter Report* meeting. He has no idea that going to Carter's program will save his life.

The man with the knife follows his victim into the hall. He sees the armed guards standing around the walls and realises he cannot kill his victim here because there's no chance to escape. He takes a seat where he can see the victim and then follow him into the night when the program ends. While waiting for the time when he can pounce, he listens to the preacher. And what the preacher says changes his thinking.

He can't believe what is happening. He no longer wants to follow his victim out of the hall. Instead he wants to stay and communicate with the preacher. He writes a note and asks someone to hand it to Carter. It reads:

Dear Pastor Carter,

I came to the meeting tonight armed with a knife. I was determined to kill a man I have been following all day. This man has done me harm and I had decided to kill him. But as you were speaking, something touched my heart. Now I am powerless to carry out my intention. I have decided to come to all the meetings to find out what message God has for me.

Astonishingly, the would-be murderer even puts his name to the letter. He is hiding nothing. He wants what Carter has to offer.

Carter shares the letter with the next morning's meeting of his 80 teenagers from Sydney. Its impact on the young people is electric. The life-and-death issues here are now starting to seem far more important than their life of criticism back home.

On another night the team receives another letter. This one is from a young pickpocket. This letter complains that fellow pickpockets have been attending the meetings and changing their ways. The writer is upset that he no longer has help when he goes along the streets to do his work.

This evangelistic series has taken most of the Aussie young people out of their comfort zone. Now they are about to go even further out of the zone.

Adventists from Manila have been regularly visiting the jail to share the gospel with its inmates. Their work has been so successful that now a Seventh-day Adventist church has begun inside the prison. The Australian young people are taken to that church. Their guide shows them blood on the floor where an inmate was murdered for coming to this church.

Carter and fellow Australian evangelist Graeme Bradford are then escorted further into the prison. They are taken to death row, where a group of eight young men are waiting for the electric chair. John speaks to them fervently, because they don't have much time left. Carter wants them to make their decisions today. He tells them that

Jesus died in a Roman "electric chair" for their sakes. He makes an appeal for those who want eternal life to raise their hands. Each prisoner sitting on those hard wooden benches raises a hand.

Then Carter asks these men on death row if they want to be baptised. They all say yes. They move to another part of the jail where an old tank with dirty water is used as a baptismal font. To Carter, the eight men look like boys, no older than 17 or 18. Carter and Bradford talk to them, and then they fully immerse each one of them. In a few weeks time, each will face the electric chair. But today they have unexpected joy in their lives that can give them life beyond that chair. Today they have accepted the promise of eternal life. Although they didn't have long to live, these eight convicted murders are enthusiastic about their new-found faith. In the few weeks before they died, they lead two other prisoners to Christ.

Several nights later Carter raises the same life-and-death issues at the International Convention Center. He asks those who want to be baptised to come forward.

This Manila campaign is a turning point for many people.

Several thousand Filipino people decide to change their lives and dedicate themselves to God.

Many of the 80 Australian young people are so affected that criticism ceases to be part of their daily life. Several of these young people decide to become ministers.

And John Carter himself is changed. He sees more clearly that his life of winning souls will no longer be only in Australia.

MARCHED INTO THE BUSH AT GUNPOINT

Few people experience the trauma of being marched at gunpoint into the bush to be shot. And even fewer live to tell the tale. John Carter had this experience in the southern African country of Zimbabwe.

The Carter family had moved to Texas, where John worked as a pastor and evangelist.

The state of Texas had the image of being the most evangelistic place in the English-speaking Adventist world. Many people there were choosing to join the Adventist Church. And many ministers of other denominations were studying their Bibles and becoming Seventh-day Adventists. For John Carter, these things made Texas an exciting place to be.

But his evangelism continued to have an international focus and this is what leads him to the continent of Africa.

Carter's program at the Harare International Conference Centre will not just be a meeting for 6000 people. Nothing like this has ever happened in Zimbabwe, so the media make it a national event.

Brochures promoting his meetings have the heading "Amazing

Discoveries in Lost Cities of the Dead." The TV ads show Carter in exotic locations in Egypt. They are the first religious TV advertisements broadcast in this part of the world. They captivate the public.

But roads in the city of Harare were not designed to cope with the large response the advertising generates. Traffic is gridlocked around the conference centre. As people abandon their cars and walk to the meetings, the area becomes a sea of humanity.

About 18,000 people attend the opening meeting, the largest attendance at an Adventist evangelistic campaign in Africa.

The meetings haven't just caught the public's imagination. They've intrigued the media as well. What Carter says each night is in newspapers and on TV the next day.

The 10th night of Carter's program is on the subject "Who is the antichrist?" Carter has a giant blackboard and very thick chalk. He opens his Bible and one by one reads out identifying marks of the antichrist. One by one he lists these identifying marks on the giant board.

1. The antichrist is a persecuting power.

2. Antichrist is combination of church and state.

3. It's a European power.

4. It changes God's laws. . . .

The list goes on until there are 14 or 15 items on the board. However, Carter doesn't name any person, nation or organisation. It is the same presentation that won him a standing ovation in the Philippines three years earlier. This year it earns him the front page of the next morning's *Harare Times*.

Carter is still asleep. But this is too important to let him doze on. Australian and American young people on his team wake him to show him the morning paper. The half-awake preacher tries to read and digest it: "The nation's Catholic bishops will hold an emergency meeting because John Carter has said the Catholic Church is the antichrist."

"That's misreporting! I didn't say that," Carter says as he comes awake. He reminds his young team members that he didn't name anyone. "I just wrote identifying marks from the Bible on the blackboard."

The Catholic bishops meet and urge the Government of Prime Minister Robert Mugabe to close down Carter's meetings. For several days there is debate across the nation.

The *Harare Times* publishes two full pages of letters on the subject. Some letters support Carter. Some oppose. Some say he should be thrown out of the country.

This is the only time in his life Carter is featured in a newspaper cartoon. The drawing shows Carter and a Catholic bishop attacking each other. The bishop is trying to hit Carter with a shepherd's crook. Carter is trying to jab him with a microphone.

Several nights after the controversy begins, a government minister arrives at Carter's meetings. Carter is about to announce the Solusi Choir when the minister walks onto the stage.

"I have an official statement to make to this meeting from the Mugabe Government," he says.

"Wait until the choir sings," Carter responds.

Members of the Carter team are afraid that Carter is about to be expelled. Senior church administrators are sitting in the front seats with worry written all over their faces.

But Carter knew in advance that the government official planned to speak to the meeting. Carter has Zimbabwe's flag displayed on the stage and he has arranged that a choir of ministerial students from the nearby Adventist college will sing a 10-minute version of the national anthem.

As they sing, the audience joins in. Black African women vibrate their hands on their mouths to make traditional African rhythms. Everyone is caught up in the spirit of patriotism. It is an emotional experience.

The government minister then asks Carter to stand beside him.

"Africa owes a great debt to the missionaries who have come to work for our people," he says. "And I thank you for coming, Pastor Carter. A genuine Christian message needs to be heard in Africa. It doesn't help when one religious group attacks another. Many people have heard that Carter is attacking others, preaching against the antichrist.

"I have been sitting in the audience every night taking notes. Now, what have I heard? I have heard the love of God, and the grace of God. I haven't heard one personal thrust or criticism. Not one word of criticism! I have only heard the living Word of God."

The government minister then turns to Carter and as he speaks he makes the sign of the cross.

"Pastor Carter, in the name of the Father, the Son and the Holy Ghost, in the name of the Government of Zimbabwe, I charge you to keep on preaching the Word of God. Do not be turned from your course.

"Preach the Word!

"Preach the Word!

"Preach the Word!"

The church officers in the front row are greatly relieved. They beam with joy. The crowd is far more emotional. They jump to their feet, and start clapping their hands and cheering wildly—and their cheers don't stop for several minutes.

After the program, the government minister has a private meeting with Carter.

"There are many people who want to argue with you," he says. "Don't argue with anybody. Don't get involved in debates. These people are troublemakers. Don't get involved with them."

Carter gives his promise. He won't argue or debate with anyone in Zimbabwe.

* * *

Two days later a TV station contacts Paula Owens, a team member from Texas who is handling the Carter program's publicity. The TV producer asks for an interview with Carter. It is a trap, but neither John nor Paula knows it, so they agree.

The government radio and TV complex is a large off-white group of buildings beyond the outskirts of the city of Harare. It has a pleasing architecture of one-, three- and four-storey buildings. Several satellite dishes and a tall red-and-white metal tower stand beside the studio complex.

Carter and Paula are greeted warmly, but soon find out they have been lured here under false pretenses. They are not here for an interview, but for a televised debate with a Catholic bishop.

John Carter is extremely courteous when he advises that he cannot take part in the debate. "I have given an undertaking to a government minister that I will not be involved in any debates."

The producer is furious Carter hasn't stepped into his trap. He calls in armed soldiers and orders Carter and Owens removed from the studio at gunpoint.

The pair is marched a short distance down the main road, then along a dirt track into the bush. The producer follows them in his white Peugeot station wagon, leaning out the window cursing and insulting them. Paula whispers to Carter, "This is no time for heroics."

There are 20 heavily armed soldiers, all have their weapons aimed at the pair. There is no chance of escape.

Carter recalls that he was extremely calm and confident. He felt God would take care of him. He genuinely wasn't afraid. He had no idea what was going to happen but he didn't believe his work for God was yet finished. So he didn't believe he was going to die—even if everything around him suggested he had only minutes to live.

After marching completely into the bush, the producer leaves Carter and Owens to their fate. He turns his car around and drives away.

The company of soldiers march the pair another 100 metres (100 yards) down the secluded track with guns still pointing at them. Then the officer orders them to stop.

A large white smile beams across the officer's big black face. "Don't worry, Pastor Carter," he says. "We attend your meetings. You are safe with us. We will defend you with our lives."

Several soldiers come and hug Carter, then do the same with Paula.

The soldiers put their rifles on their shoulders and protectively march Carter and Paula to an army post. There they telephone David Carter to come and take the pair back to the city.

While he is driving to pick up his father, soldiers with submachine guns fire multiple rounds over the roof of David's car. However, he reaches his father unscathed, and takes him back to the city.

John arrives at the convention centre half-an-hour late. Despite the ordeal, he walks onto the stage and delivers his message as normal.

The team plans a baptism on the last Saturday of their program. About 500 people are to be fully immersed. They build their own swimming pool for the purpose. They erect a frame, cover it with rubberised cloth, and fill it with water.

The baptisms are speeded up by having several new Christians enter the water at the same time. Even so, the baptismal service takes the whole of Saturday afternoon.

John Carter leaves the country and a few weeks later several hundred more people who came to his meetings will also be baptised. But with this success comes notoriety. Carter has no idea how far and wide the events in Harare are known.

Almost every night Zimbabwe TV carried news reports of Carter's meeting. These news reports were also broadcast in Europe, elsewhere in Africa and in Australia.

✳ ✳ ✳

A few months after the Harare meetings, John Carter is the evening speaker each night for a week at Minneapolis. It is 100 years since the Adventist Church held a top-level administrative conference in this city. The 1888 conference is known for leading to a revival of righteousness by faith in the Adventist Church.

Because this was so significant, the church is holding a commemorative conference here 100 years later. Carter is the main evening speaker.

On the day the meetings start, a senior administrator arranges to meet Carter in his hotel room. Dr Bert Beach is the church's religious liberty advocate. He also represents the Adventist Church at the Holy See and with many other religious groups. He has just returned from the Vatican.

"The Pope is very unhappy with you," Beach tells Carter. "Because of the problems you caused in Zimbabwe, he's had to delay his visit there by six months."

TESTING THE WATERS IN MOSCOW

In 1990, the world leaders of the Seventh-day Adventist Church suspect the USSR may soon open up to Christianity. But they have no idea if an American preacher would be accepted in the USSR. There is a new era of openness in government. But are the attitudes of the public also changing?

Leading Adventist evangelist Pastor Robert Spangler travels to Russia to test the waters. He holds a few meetings for church members and the general public. The American is astonished by the positive response.

He returns home to Washington, DC, where he works at the world headquarters of the Seventh-day Adventist Church. In January 1991, he picks up his phone and dials the West Coast.

John and Beverley Carter are still asleep in Los Angeles. "It's Bob Spangler here, John," the voice on the phone says. "The brethren would like you to go across to Moscow, run a series of meetings, and see what sort of response you get."

"Who's going to pay for this?" Carter asked.

"You're a good fundraiser. You go ahead and do what you do well.

You raise the money for it."

Within a couple of weeks, Carter had the money. It will be the same pattern for the next 15 years. Carter will have to pay for every evangelistic series he ever runs in Russia. As a pastor, his wages will be paid by the church, but he will have to pay all other expenses himself. Of the thousands of evangelists employed by the Adventist Church worldwide, Carter is one of only a handful who doesn't receive a campaign budget from the church.

Carter, his wife, Beverley, a *Carter Report* cameraman, and two friends from Texas, Dr Russell and Paula Owens, arrive in Moscow. It is April 1991, a Thursday, two days before the meetings are due to start. Carter is still affected by jet lag and is about to face the most gruelling preaching schedule of his life.

Things are rapidly changing in Moscow. The Soviet Union is about to break into 15 independent republics. There has been widespread dissatisfaction with Communism for many years. But this is the first time people have been able to express their dissatisfaction without being sent to jail.

During the Communist era, the authorities would not let Protestants build new churches. So it was rather convenient that Adventists hold their worship services on Saturday. The Adventists were able to use a church building on Saturday, and another denomination could use the same building on Sunday.

The day after Carter arrives in Moscow, he holds a Friday-night meeting for Adventist Church members in the Moscow Baptist church. It becomes the only venue where both Carter and the great Baptist evangelist Billy Graham have spoken.

A rule of the Communist era still binding in 1991 is that churches are allowed to hold only one meeting a day. So Carter's Saturday and Sunday meetings will run nonstop from 10 am to 10 pm. On weeknights he will preach three hours each evening. In 10 days he will take 10 meetings, but he will preach for an astounding 60 hours. Yet his voice never fails.

The Russian church leaders have booked a small hall by Russian standards. It is the Palace of Culture, near the Kremlin in the centre of Moscow, seating 1800 people. It is shabby, utilitarian, run-down and needs refurbishing. But its poor quality doesn't deter the crowds. At every meeting the venue is packed. Probably 25 per cent are Christians and the rest are from the general public, most of them atheists.

Carter and his translator start preaching at 10 am and stop at 12.30 pm. They have a meal while a choir sings. Legally, the meeting hasn't stopped because the choir is singing, so there is still only one meeting for the day. Carter resumes preaching until 6 pm when he has another meal break and the choir sings again. Then he preaches until 10 pm. The audience stays for the whole 12-hour program.

At 10 pm, when the meeting is due to end, the people don't want to go home. Someone suggests they hold a question-and-answer session. About 100 people stand in a line across the stage while the audience listens. One after another they ask questions like, "What does God look like?" "Who was Jesus?" and "Did Jesus really rise from the dead?" Carter answers each question in turn. Wherever possible, he doesn't give his own opinion. He has a Bible in his hand and he reads a Bible verse to answer the question.

After almost an hour, a man comes to the head of the line and says, "I am Professor Vladim from Moscow University. I am an atheist. But I want you to tell me how to find God."

"Come to the meetings," Carter tells him. "I will give you a Bible. I want to show you evidence from archaeology, history and prophecy that there is a Creator God who loves you."

The next person in the line is someone known to everyone in the audience. "I am Andre from *Good Evening Moscow,*" says the well-known TV presenter. "We want to interview you. When can I talk to you?"

"What sort of program is it?" Carter asks.

"It's an hour-long news show each night of the week. It is shown right across the Soviet Union."

"I can't talk tonight," says Carter. "Come to the Budapest Hotel on Monday and we can discuss it."

After 13 hours on his feet, he can barely stand up to answer more questions. At last his tired feet are saved when the janitor insists on turning out the lights.

The Budapest Hotel is old and ornate. It was built in the era of the Tsars. Its bedrooms have six-metre (20-foot) high ceilings. Each room has polished wooden floors and two narrow beds with thin mattresses. The pillows are thick but the bath towels are paper thin.

Carter is waiting at the Budapest Hotel at the appointed time for the TV presenter to arrive. But Andre doesn't just come by himself. A dozen others from the TV station are with him. Carter talks with them about the importance of Christianity. They arrange a time to record the interview. The TV crew leaves. But Carter still has no idea what they are planning for the interview. *Do they want to uplift Christianity or tear it down? Is he doing the right thing to go on TV at this time? Could he be walking into another trap like the trap at the Zimbabwe TV station?*

"Our guest this evening on *Good Evening Moscow* is Pastor John Carter, a Christian minister from Australia. Welcome to *Good Evening Moscow.*"

"I'm very pleased to be here," Carter replies. Both his words in

English and the interviewer's words in Russian are translated so they can understand each other.

"You are running meetings in our city," says the interviewer. "Now, our nation is in a great state of crisis. Tell us what you think we should do.

"In 1917 we rejected God. We can now see that everything has gone bad. We want you to tell the Russian people what we can do to improve our way of life."

Carter replies, "Where the Bible goes, it lifts up society. It brings spiritual, social and psychological benefits to the people. The most backward countries of the world are the countries that reject the God of the Bible. The most prosperous countries of the world are those that follow the teachings of the Creator."

The questions keep coming. "How can we find God?" "Why do you believe that Communism is wrong?" and "Can we, the Russian people, redeem the awful mistakes of the past 70 years?"

John Carter's message is going to homes that speak Russian right across Europe and Asia. He is given 15 minutes to uplift the value of Christianity.

Normally, when a TV interview ends, a lone production assistant will come to the guests to escort them out of the studio. But after this interview, about 15 staff members gather around Carter. This interview has had a great impact, even on the TV crew.

"How many of you here are believers?" Carter asks them. All of them shake their heads, not a single hand is raised.

"I would like to do something for you. I'd like to introduce you to the Creator God. I'm going to have a prayer with you and teach you how to pray. I want you to all come together now. I want you to bow your heads and close your eyes so we can concentrate." The group gathers in a small circle on the vast TV studio floor. Carter then says a prayer asking God to bless each one of them.

"There was a great attitude of love in the room," Carter says, recounting what happened. "I was stunned and amazed. You could feel the love. One by one they hugged me. They thanked me. And they blessed me."

The Russian TV staff then call out, "Praise God!" This is a traditional Russian shout of joy from the era of the Tsars. Even when Communism took over the nation, the cry "Praise God" remained in use, although it lost its religious connotations. But now when the TV crew calls out "Praise God," it perhaps has added meaning.

The 15-minute interview is broadcast the following night. About 50 million viewers see this strong message on the value of Christianity. The leaders and members of the churches here have never seen anything like this before. They are completely stunned. The Russian church leaders say they feel like men in a dream.

Carter's instructions when he was sent to Russia were that he was not to baptise anyone. But the crowd keeps coming back to meeting after meeting. The people have now attended more than 50 hours of Christian Bible-study programs. Even though it's all happened in 10 days, it's as much as people normally hear in a full evangelistic campaign in the United States or Australia. He feels God's Spirit is prompting him to make an altar call.

About 2000 people have crowded into Moscow's Palace of Culture. Among those who cannot find a seat are a group of soldiers and their officer. Each night they have stood across the back of the hall.

Carter asks people walk to the stage to show they want to renounce sin and give their lives to God. Many people respond to the call, but he particularly notices the soldiers. Everyone else merely walks to the front. The soldiers march goosestep. Their arms swing as high as their shoulders. Carter beckons for them to march up onto the stage and they fall in line behind him.

This is not just a performance or a pantomime. The soldiers are deeply moved. They even start crying. People stream out of their seats and down to the front. Igor—Carter's translator—is so emotional he cannot speak. He's crying too. The whole audience is weeping. There is a great hush in the hall.

Nothing is said for five minutes. The only sound is widespread sobbing. Carter is crying also.

"This is the first time I have seen this. This is the first time," says Igor, thinking this must be common in the West. But this is probably the first time anyone anywhere has seen a meeting stop for five minutes of crying. "It is a new day for us," says Igor.

Igor later writes an article about this. It is called "Ten days that changed Russia." He chooses that title because 10 days also changed Russia in the revolution of 1917. He shows that the impact of Carter's 10 days of preaching was felt far beyond the walls of the Palace of Culture. Thanks to his TV interview, Carter's impact has been taken to every corner of the Soviet empire. He was just a preacher, doing a job for God. But in that 10 days he made an impact that claimed a place for Christianity in the 15 new nations that will form in a few months time. (While Carter did not baptise anyone in Moscow, 100 people who had attended his meetings were baptised three months after he left.)

Mikhail Kulakov is one of those who witnessed the amazing five minutes of sobbing. His father had been a Seventh-day Adventist pastor during the Communist era. One day the authorities came and took his father away. That was the last time the family saw him.

Despite this experience, Mikhail chose to follow his father's footsteps. As a result he spent five years in a harsh Communist jail. Now, in the last years of the Soviet Union, he has become the president of the Adventist Church for the whole of the USSR.

Mikhail is astonished by the Carter meetings. He gathers other senior officials of the Russian Adventist Church, and then he contacts Carter.

"The brethren want you to come back for a big campaign," he says. "The Russian church asks you to come."

"Where will we hold it?" Carter asks.

The church president replies, "Maybe we could get the Great Hall of Congress in the Kremlin." When the church leaders book the Kremlin for Carter's meetings, it makes news around the world. Christians are going to hold evangelistic meetings in the citadel of Communism.

This simple news item had an incredible impact on Christianity, alerting Christians all over the world to consider evangelism in Russia. So Carter didn't just "test the waters" for the Seventh-day Adventist Church. In a way he tested the waters for all Christian churches.

While this news item announced that Carter was booked to preach at the Kremlin, it never happened. Another evangelist led that series while Carter went to run a program in the Russian city of Gorky.

In Gorky, he baptised 2530 people. He returned to the same city the following year, ran another evangelistic series, and baptised 1500 more new Christians. And he returned the year after that with a series that baptised another 1300. In all, Carter's programs in that city baptised more than 6000 people, with about 2000 more people who attended his meetings being baptised in follow-up programs.

In about four years, a city with 120 church members grew to a membership of about 10,000.

INSIGHTS FROM A CLOSE FRIEND

Graeme Bradford was a leading evangelist in Australia who became a lecturer at Avondale College. He has been one of John Carter's closest friends and confidants for 25 years. When Carter held his first major campaign in Russia, he asked Bradford to be the team manager.

Bradford provides a unique perspective on John Carter. He has known him for almost 50 years and, as a top-flight evangelist himself, he has a better understanding of the mindset of a fellow evangelist.

When did you first meet John?

We were students at college together. I started there as a student in 1960 when John was in the third year of the ministerial course. He was one of a very talented class that graduated in 1961.

So what was he like then?

He was always enthusiastic. He always worked hard at anything he did. He was one of our better preachers and speakers. When he preached, he preached enthusiastically. He put his whole heart in it.

He worked very hard in his preaching. I enjoyed it.

I used to see him sitting on the lawn talking to Bev Buchanan, his wife's name before they married. John has been given a wonderful wife. She's a rare person. She's a gem.

To be an evangelist's wife takes a very special type of woman. There's the continual moving from home to home. There's the pressure of the program. People let you down. Things don't work as they should. An evangelist's wife lives through all this pressure too.

You have to say that Bev is a significant part of John's success. She understands him. She is very loyal. She's very supportive. I don't think John could have achieved near what he has achieved if God hadn't given him the right wife. I think it's God's plan they got together. She is so committed to winning people to Christ.

I've never seen them anything but happy and united. I think they've done very well together.

You have worked with John as his campaign manager.

The first one I worked on with him was the one in Manila [in the Philippines].

How did that happen? How did you have time available?

I was a union evangelist in Adelaide at the time. John asked me if I would come and help him.

I asked [the union president] Claude Judd if it was a good idea. He said, "Yes. John needs someone who can organise things, so you had better go and help him."

I was given permission by [the church administrators in] South Australia to take the time off to go and be with him.

This was the first time you sat in on a Carter series. As one of his peers, what was your view of John's program?

I enjoyed it because I enjoy his preaching. There are very few people I like listening to on a regular basis. But I like his oratory, his preaching. It's no hardship to sit and listen to him preach. It's good.

Since then you have worked with John on a number of his campaigns. You must have had some "interesting" experiences?

There have been many crises. When we were in Jamaica, we had all of John's [photographic] slides in the roof-rack of a bus. They tried to drive the bus into the stadium to unload his pictures and his projectors for use in the program. It was a stupid thing to do because the bus became jammed [against the roof of the tunnel]. It was just a little while before the program was due to start and here's John's pictures and equipment jammed in the roof-rack at the top of the bus. They eventually got it down. Then the program started and one of the projectors blew. Yet despite all those obstacles, the program went ahead.

John's usual way of greeting me, whether it's Manila, Jamaica, Australia, Russia or wherever I am working with him, is not "G'day, Graeme, how are you going?" His usual greeting is, "Graeme, we have a major crisis on our hands."

When John arrived at Nizhni Novgorod [for his first major series in Russia], I came down to greet him. His first words were, "Graeme we have a major crisis on our hands. Our equipment is stuck in London and we can't get it through." This sort of thing happens on a regular, day-by-day basis with him. Yet, whether it's God's intervention, answer to prayer or John's sheer cussedness, the fact is, he always seems to get there. This is an amazing thing about him. It blows me apart; absolutely blows me apart.

I've had more excitement, drama, intrigue and absolute thrills working with John [than at any other time in my life].

Tell me about your experience in the Manila jail.

John and I went into the high-security section of the jail where the prisoners were about to be put to death. We asked each of these guys why they were there. It was for murder. When we baptised them, you could feel their bodies tremble as they went under the water. It meant so much to them.

John told the prisoners the story of Harry Orchard [an American in prison for murdering the State Governor of Idaho]. He told them how in prison Harry Orchard became a Christian, became a Seventh-day Adventist. The prisoners listened as John told them about God's love, mercy and goodness. John made an appeal. The prisoners put their hands through the bars to respond, to accept the appeal, to accept Christ. That was very moving.

The jail visit was filmed by a local TV station. It went all across the nation on the news that night. It was incredible.

They filmed the baptism?

Yes. We had a TV crew in there with us. There were two baptisms, one in the minimum-security section where we baptised a couple of hundred. Every member of the Adventist Church there was a criminal. The church clerk was in there for fraud.

There was also a baptism in the high-security section. When we went in, we wondered why the guards didn't come with us. The guards left us at the gate because inside there were killings, rapes, butchering, drugs, knives. That's what they did. They butchered each other. That's what prison life was like. The guards didn't go in there. They showed us the place inside a building that was used for a church where our church treasurer had been murdered a week or so earlier. On the way out, the guards said, "We didn't want to tell you this until now, but last week some Baptist missionaries were taken hostage when they went in there. But we thought we'd better not tell you until you came out."

John has a lot of courage. He takes on dangerous situations. I've never known him to take a backward step in difficult situations.

Tell me about when you were manager of John's campaign in Jamaica.

That was after Manila. I had started teaching at Avondale College. A team of young folk came across with us. We ran in a huge outdoor football stadium so there were nights when John had to preach in the pouring rain. Tom Mitchell was playing the piano totally covered by a tarpaulin. Warren Judd's orchestra took shelter by playing underneath the stage.

I remember handing John the microphone one night, telling him to be careful that he wasn't electrocuted. Electricity is pretty dangerous stuff in the rain.

I don't think the Jamaicans had done the preparation that the Filipino people had. When we got to the Philippines, we could see the advertising all over the city. They had really prepared the territory well. But the Jamaicans hadn't.

We had music before the program started. And the Adventist Jamaicans were so lively. They would probably embarrass the Charismatics in Australia or America. You should see the way they worship! You see a stadium with 20,000 people waving their hands up and down singing songs. And the local Jamaicans leading the singing of the songs bounced around on the stage almost like a band at a dance.

How did the Jamaicans react to John's preaching?

Before we left, one of the Jamaican pastors made a speech. He said in front of all the other pastors, "I thought that the era of great preaching was finished and gone. But now I have heard John Carter, I believe there are still great preachers around." The most important tribute I have ever heard to John's preaching was made by that guy—because the Jamaicans themselves are very good preachers. They are very lively. They have good content. So I felt it was a very nice tribute.

You were also manager of John's first campaign in Russia.

Five months before that program started, John and I went there to organise it. It was between 15 and 20 degrees below freezing. The Volga River had frozen right across. There was a shortage of food. People stood in long lines to buy food they couldn't afford. It was reported that people were dying in the food lines. They were taking the people to the morgue with their bodies frozen, still clutching their shopping bags. The aged, the infirm—these were the ones who were dying.

John and I went down the street and we saw people lined up to buy fish. At that time the Russian currency had slipped to 300 roubles for one American dollar. When I did my first trip there, it had been one dollar for one ruble. So John bought the entire truckload of fish and gave it to the people [in the line]. The folk were absolutely bewildered.

Tell me about your meetings with the church members.

John collected money from his church in Los Angeles and we had a Sabbath meeting with our people [in Gorky]. John had converted the money into roubles and we put the money into envelopes and put the envelopes in an offering plate. The plate went around and people were able to take an envelope. The money in the envelope was a love gift from their fellow Adventists in America to help them get through the winter. Watching them receive this was a very moving experience.

I took a Friday-night meeting and the division president, Mikhail Kulakov, translated for me. They had a prayer season at the end, and Kulakov was whispering the translation of the prayers in my ear. The prayers were like David in the psalms. It was the most moving prayer season I have heard in my life. "Lord, don't forget us." "Don't forget we need you." "Help us. We need to get through this winter."

It brought tears to my eyes. It was very, very moving to hear our people pleading with God to be able to get through the winter alive.

The next day that money from John's American church was given out [in the church service]. That was such a wonderful thing for those people.

So what were the expectations in Nizhni Novgorod?

When John and I first went there, there was [only] one church there. Neal Wilson [the General Conference president] had said to me, "You ought to run there because we have a new church building. It seats about 160 people, and we have 100-odd Adventists there, so you have a place to put new people. He was thinking we would win 30, 40 or 50 new people.

In the end it was 2530 by John's count.

I came back a few months later and baptised another couple of hundred. And there were other baptisms afterwards too. I think the final figure was closer to 3000.

At the time, you were worried about keeping the new converts in the church. What did you do about it?

I went back and ran a follow-up series for 10 days. [Australian evangelist] Lindsay Laws and his wife, June, went there to help with the follow-up after we left. We did the best we could to give instruction [to the new converts]. The trouble is there were not enough pastors to care for them. The pastors we did have didn't have cars [to visit the new members' homes]. And we didn't have church buildings.

Tell me about the first baptism in Russia.

Baptism meant so much to the people. It was a way of binding them to us and to the church.

The army set up the tents for me. There were 30 or 40 pastors in the water. You don't see that too often. That baptism we had of 1800 people in one day—I could never forget that day. I must have baptised a few hundred myself. I finished up baptising people two at a time, a husband and a wife together, two young people together. That was a thrill. John didn't get into the water to baptise. He stood on the shore. The reason for that is that if he had been in the water doing the baptising, they would have all lined up to be baptised by him. As it was, a huge number lined up to be baptised by me because I was the second in charge.

There was another baptism at Nizhni when protestors came out to prevent the baptism. The Orthodox Church brought all these protestors out to stop the baptism. John had David Carter up in a helicopter flying overhead to make a video of the baptism. It was an army helicopter. The protestors saw the helicopter flying overhead and they said, "Oh, he's got the military on his side." And they turned around and dissolved away.

What interesting incidents happened in the first campaign?

Did John tell you about how they broke a hole in the wall to get in? They were lined up at the first meeting and were determined to get in. So they made a hole in the wall to get inside.

Tell me about giving out the Bibles there.

We stamped the back of people's hands to show they had received a Bible because some people were doubling up to get more than one. Some people found a way of removing that stamp from the back of their hand. We gave away 25,000 Bibles. Some people treasured their Bible. They loved it. You could see it meant a lot to them. But you will always get an element in society who will try to take advantage of the situation. And the local black market was flooded with Bibles.

You had Mafia at the meetings.

Yes. The local pastors told us, "The Mafia are here!" The Mafia then contacted us and said, "We will protect you for a certain amount of money." You know what that means. If you don't pay us, we'll do you in. They were quite capable of kidnapping us, or kidnapping some of the wealthy Americans [on the team]. We negotiated with the KGB. John paid them $200 American. That was a lot of money to them. It was 60,000 roubles. The KGB then turned up at the meetings and they got rid of the Mafia.

Where did you keep the money to run the program?

John had it around his waist in a big, fat money-belt. He looked like he had a big waistline. And as the campaign progressed, he got thinner.

It doesn't seem like a safe idea. If the Mafia had found out, he would have been killed.

You couldn't trust the banks in Russia.

What's John like to work with?

You're not going to ruin my good friendship with him, are you?

Absolutely, I am.

He lives under a lot of tension and pressure. There is always pressure. I think one reason John and I worked well together was that being an evangelist, I probably understood better than most the pressure he was under.

To me, the worst part of a series is the first night when you're waiting to see if anyone is going to turn up. You've done your homework. What will happen?

Let's face it; a lot of people are waiting to tear evangelists apart. They have their calculators out, adding up how much money has been spent, and saying, "Where is the return?"

I could identify with John when he faced pressures like that.

John gets very tense and very tight before a meeting. If a meeting has gone well, his body language certainly reveals that.

Why has he been so successful?

There are many reasons. Not the least is that fact that when he preaches he is always conscious of the need to make the good news about Jesus prominent. People who respond to his preaching become conscious of the gospel. It features prominently in their thinking. They keep wanting to talk about the goodness of God.

John warms the hearts of the people with the fact that God loves them and wants to give them eternal life as a free gift. In the developing world where legalism seems to flourish, it seemed to come across as something few had ever heard before. Certainly they were not getting it from the larger established churches, which were steeped in ritualism.

John's local church in California gives incredible support.

Although this church numbers only a few hundred people, they give $500,000 each year toward his ministry. They love his preaching and yet they are prepared to see him go away for months at a time to raise up new churches. I have never seen another church so focused on getting out the Adventist message.

Over a period of 15 years, I have preached in this church when John has been away running his campaigns. It is always a delight to preach there because the people are so responsive to preaching.

Their support for his ministry is incredible. When you are among them they want to keep talking about evangelism. It is really interesting to be in the church on Sabbath morning when they contact John by phone and get the latest reports on his [overseas] programs. There is an air of expectation as the phone rings and rejoicing when they hear the news.

If we had more Adventist churches with this church's spirit and level of commitment, how quickly the Adventist message would spread.

John has inspired many young ministers.

John came to Avondale College and spoke to my ministerial students about a year-and-a-half ago. In the space of an hour-and-a-half, he fired them up. Those students will never forget it. He told them where he'd been, what he'd done. The students were just blown away. They'd never heard anyone speak like this before.

John is a visionary. I don't know anyone else who is so able to motivate people. He can get people to come with him halfway around the world. He can raise half a million dollars, transport all his people, get a thing going. That's a tremendous achievement, isn't it. When you think what he has done and what he has achieved, I think it's incredible. Look at his achievements. How many other people could do that?

There will always be some people who will oppose and criticise what he has done. Let them equal his achievements. I don't see the critics doing anything like the good he has achieved. You would have to say that God has blessed the way John has been used to bring people to know Christ. In the end, that's what matters.

I thank God for the privilege of working with John. I really do.

JOHN CARTER'S GREATEST WEAKNESSES?

J ohn Carter himself identifies a love of good cars as one of his greatest weaknesses. He drives three hours on clogged California freeways almost every working day. Having a good car reduces his stress levels at work and at home.

"Most people perceive me as being *very* independent," Carter says, emphasising the word *very*. "This has come back to me [from church administrators] a million times." However, of those who know him personally, not a single one mentions independence as a weakness. They usually see this as one of his strengths.

"One of my church members bumped into Neal Wilson [the former world leader of the Adventist Church] in Washington, DC. She asked, 'Do you know John Carter?' Neal replied, 'Yes, of course I know him. He's known around the world. I like him. But he's very independent.'

"Among Adventist administrators, to be called *independent* is worse than being called a fornicator," Carter says with a laugh.

"My biggest failure in life has been not to spend enough time with my kids when they were young. My biggest single failure was doing what the church administration told me to do and to move to a different place every year. My wife handled it pretty well, but it was not fair to my children and I regret it. I should have had more common sense and thought more about the welfare of my children. I can remember my daughter, Leanne, vomiting when she had to start a new school every year. My biggest failure was not to put them first, and that's something I will always regret.

"My biggest weakness is impatience," Carter says. "Short term I'm impatient. Long term, I'm patient. It has been said I don't suffer fools gladly. I am very impatient with people working for me who do dumb and stupid things. But I try to take a long-term view of people's wellbeing and not do anything that's going to hurt them.

"Another weakness is that I know what it is to get depressed. I sympathise with Winston Churchill, and with Martin Luther who [when he was depressed] threw an inkwell at the devil."

His periods of depression usually last only a few days. "They usually come after a big campaign, when I'm drained emotionally and in every other way. Elijah had it, you know. After the success of Mount Carmel, he was depressed." The phenomenon of being depressed after completing a *successful* project may seem unusual. But psychiatrists report that it's surprisingly common.

Both Carter and those who know him list being unapproachable as a significant weakness. However, it's more a matter of timing. There are times when he is approachable, and certain fixed times when he's not. "After a big meeting, I really don't want to be approached. I've poured out everything and there's not much left to be poured out. A bad time to approach me is before or after a sermon. Before a meeting I'm like a racehorse at a barrier ready to go. After the meeting, I'm usually spent."

Carter points to other evangelists who had the same experience. "You've heard of Billy Sunday. After a big campaign they had to treat him like a dying man for weeks because he had expended so much energy. The book *The Desire of Ages* suggests that even our Lord was totally exhausted after the big meetings He took. Billy Graham, after he ran meetings, used to go into the hills in Carolina. And Fordyce Detamore, the great American Adventist evangelist, would hold three weeks of meetings then go waterskiing on a lake.

"If it's a really big meeting, I am on an emotional and spiritual high and I don't want to stand around talking to people. I want to get away by myself and preferably go for a long walk."

As well as asking Carter about his weaknesses, many of his staff suggested similar weaknesses. One unusual weakness was reported by Misty Stiles, the manager of *The Carter Report* office.

"I would say [that his greatest weakness], and I know that this is a strength in some areas, is his [extreme] capacity to forgive. He has this patient attitude of allowing people to grow. But sometimes you meet people who are predators, and John will allow this—trying to extend them a hand, trying to give them an opportunity. But sometimes you can see that it takes a toll on him from a stress point of view.

"Another weakness would be that the guy has a lot of compassion. For him, this can translate into stress. It's a lot to carry on one person's shoulders. After a lot of trips to Russia, you would think he would be used to it. But after 29 trips, you can still see that he wants to cry over what he has seen there. He feels things too deeply."

"He's a workaholic," says Donn Beagle, who does audio work for Carter's evangelistic series and for his radio and TV programs.

Susan Pirano, who's worked for Carter for 13 years, agrees.

"Sometimes he can push himself too hard," she says. "Let's say there is a campaign we are planning and we have to raise half a million dollars. He will keep pushing himself to get the money. I say to him, 'Sometimes you have to wait and see what the Lord will do.'

"I think that he doesn't take enough time to enjoy things. He's so busy going from one thing to the other. You have to stop and smell the roses. I think he has come to realise this over the years."

Susan sees that the same instant outcomes that he wants from himself and sometimes from God, Carter also wants from his staff. "He wants immediate results [from his staff], and sometimes that just can't happen, no matter how hard you try," Susan says.

David Carter, who produces Carter's TV programs, agrees. "We are going to Egypt [producing TV programs] in four weeks time. Dad hasn't allowed us time to do the preparation that needs to be done."

But after saying that, David is quick to spring to his father's defence. "I don't want to be seen as saying anything negative about my father. I don't *have* to work here. I *chose* to work here. I want to help my parents because they are naive enough to believe they can make the world a better place. And they have. One thing I have learned from my parents is that one person can make a difference. A lot of people in this world throw their hands up and say 'What can one person do?' But if you go to Russia and ask 'Can one person make a difference?' thousands of Russians would say yes. In many parts of Russia, Dad is a hero."

Perhaps we should leave the final word on this subject to Sandy Hou, a production assistant on *The Carter Report* TV program. "I've been here only three-and-a-half years and I don't know of any weaknesses," she says. "The staff don't complain about John—at least, not that I know of."

May 2006

AN INTERVIEW WITH A WARRIOR

E vangelism in Russia was actually a "sideline" for John Carter. During the 15 years he preached in the former USSR, he was officially a local church pastor in California. After 43 years in the ministry, he retired as a pastor in 2004. But retirement hasn't stopped him preaching. He hopes it will give him more time for his first love, being an evangelist.

Carter leans back in his chair, in a mood to reminisce. A smile creeps over his face.

Why are you suddenly smiling?

I was remembering flying over Siberia in an old Russian twin-engine passenger aircraft. It was 2003. Four stewardesses were chatting and glancing toward me. Then one of them then came over and asked, "Excuse me. Are you John Carter?"

I replied, "Yes, I am."

She said, "I want to thank you for what you are doing for our country."

It totally caught me by surprise. The three other hostesses joined in and echoed her remarks. You don't do what I have done to receive thanks on this earth. But it warms your heart when it comes your way, just out of the blue.

And your evangelism has also touched world leaders.

Yes. The Governor-General of one country asked me to visit him for a private meeting, which I did. I've discussed Christianity in private conversations with senior Russian politicians.

In another country the Prime Minister came to my program one night. The next morning I had a phone call from his private secretary, who said the Prime Minister wanted to come and see me privately. I was staying in rather shabby accommodation, not suitable to host the visit of a prime minister. So I said I would go and see the Prime Minister. I went to his official residence.

He said, "I listened to your program on John 3:16 last night. It touched my heart. I went home and got my Bible and searched it for hours. I really needed that."

The Prime Minister and I had a good long talk on spiritual matters. He hugged me. And I prayed with him. He invited me to come back and run another campaign in his country. He said that if I came back, he would be willing to be the master of ceremonies for my series and he would personally bring people to the meetings.

Unfortunately, my schedule did not take me back to his country.

Tell me about the newspaper wanting you to be the mayor.

It wasn't the mayor, it was governor—in Gorky in 1992. They said that if I ran for governor, I would probably be elected. And it was probably true.

How much time have you actually spent in the former USSR?

It almost seems as if it's a lifetime. In reality, the total time I've spent in those countries is only two-and-a-half years.

You've achieved all that in two-and-a-half years?

Yes, by God's grace.

You've had interesting experiences with the Mafia.

The Russian Mafia make the American Mafia look like gentlemen at a church picnic. When our historic meetings were underway in Nizhni Novgorod during 1992, we stayed at the Russia Hotel, a meeting place for the Mafia. We watched them doing business, coming and going.

Then one day they sent me a message: "We want to meet with you." Invariably, such meetings are to demand protection money. So instead of meeting with them, we sent a message to the governor. That night, when we arrived at the 'Russia' after the meetings, we found the hotel surrounded by members of the Special Security Forces armed to the teeth. The Mafia men were being taken away handcuffed.

About the same time, Mafia mobsters threatened our church's seminary at Tula, near Moscow. They demanded large amounts of money to "protect" the college. They gave the leaders of the seminary a day or two to think it over. Then they promised that they would be back to take delivery.

The gangsters got in their car and drove off. Just a little way down the road they were killed in a car accident. It's a dangerous business to threaten God's people, no matter how tough you think you are.

You have a lot of help from church members in your work.

More than 500 church members, aged from eight to 80, have gone with us to help our programs in Russia and Ukraine. They've come from Australia, New Zealand, the United States, Canada, South Africa and a few from elsewhere. Without these people we couldn't have accomplished one-tenth of what happened.

Some pastors went through tough times under Communism.

I think most of them did. Take the example Pastor Murgar, who was president of the Christian Adventist Church in Ukraine when I held my 1995 campaign in Kiev.

During the Communist era, Murgar had been sentenced to five years jail with hard labour. While there he was beaten, starved and went through frequent torture sessions. He was a Christian minister and the KGB wanted him to inform on church members. When he wouldn't do it, they threw him in jail. They would starve him and torture him, then offer to release him if he would spy on his church members. He wouldn't budge, so they would lock him up again. Then they would go through the same sequence of depravation, torture, then a promise of release. He stayed in prison until the death of Stalin. I call him "a hero of the faith."

How do you have so much energy when you preach?

I will tell you a personal story, but I don't want people to think I am a nut. I have known the ecstasy of angels, and the blackest moments of despair. I have experienced times of real depression. Often I have no energy while I am waiting to walk on the stage. Then as I have walked on the stage, it is as if a mantle falls on me. I am a different person. I have tremendous energy. The words just flow out, I don't have to think. My mind is running ahead of my mouth. When it's all over and I walk off the stage, the power goes.

What do you do to stay healthy?

I exercise every day. Every day I either use the Nordic Trac cross-country skier or I walk for one or two hours. If I didn't exercise, I'd be dead.

You like to take a walk after you preach.

Yes. I walk hard. It gives my mind a chance to wind down. When I'm preaching, my mind is usually running faster than my mouth. I have 1000 thoughts running through my mind. After I preach, you just can't turn that off. It takes me a while to wind down. Walking helps me wind down.

What about your diet?

I am very careful about what I eat. I eat plenty of fruit. I eat oatmeal, soy milk, tofu, salsa, vegetables. I eat lots of almonds, wholemeal bread. I don't eat butter or anything like that.

It's been 50 years since I last ate red meat. I gave up meat when I was 17, when I went to Avondale College. I haven't eaten it since.

A week ago you said you were going though the worst crisis in your life.

My doctor called me [after a regular medical check-up] with some concern. There is a bit of plaque in two of my heart arteries. That, of course, has the potential of causing a heart attack. Previously, I had been told [by my doctor, that] my heart was good, so this has come as a shock.

It was the last thing I expected to hear. [*Carter pauses and smiles slightly.*] It's been caused by stress. But the doctors say it appears my exercise program and my dietary habits have preserved my life.

What has this health crisis been like for you?

It's been a time of reflection. A time of seeking God. A time of appreciation. I went down to the park the other day and walked around it. I saw the children playing. I looked at the wonderful blue sky and the beautiful green trees. I felt the whisper of a breeze and thought to myself, *How blessed I am just to be alive.*

During all of this [health crisis] I've had a remarkable peace. I believe that God is in charge. I've done all I can humanly speaking to obey his laws concerning my health. Therefore, I can leave it all in His hands, knowing whatever comes from His hands is good.

Because they have to preach on Sabbath, many pastors take another day off to reduce their stress. Do you do that?

I used to take Mondays off when I was a young minister in Australia. I haven't been doing it for a long time. But because of my heart scare, I'm going to start taking a regular day off again.

I don't think you are a perfectionist by nature, but you have made yourself a perfectionist.

I don't have a lot of empathy with people who have the notion that what you do for God is throwing Him the leftovers. I find that idea disconcerting. I will not work with people who have that attitude.

If you could ask God three questions, what would they be?

I'm not too much into asking God questions. I saw a plaque in the Garden of Gethsemane that said, "We may not understand you

[God], but we don't have to."

One day in glory, however, I would like to ask the Lord some questions that pertain to science, where there appears to be conflict with orthodox Christianity.

How many of your evangelistic campaigns have failed?

I have never run an evangelistic campaign that hasn't been fruitful. So I would say I've never had an evangelistic campaign that's been a failure. Glory be to God!

When and where was your first evangelistic campaign?

It was in 1965 in Parkes, the geographic centre of New South Wales, Australia. It had a population of 8500. We held the meetings in the Orange Hall, which was no longer used. The church ladies used to remove the bird droppings off the stage each Sunday and scrub it clean each week.

When I decided to hold two sessions of the opening meeting, the church members thought I had either great faith or great stupidity. But we had about 85 or 90 people at each session.

We baptised about a dozen brand-new people, which was the most ever in the town. The church had about 60 members, so it was a 20 per cent increase.

Where was your next campaign?

It was in a town near Parkes called Forbes. We didn't have a church in that town. We baptised 12 or 13 people. That was a lot harder than baptising 2000 people in Russia.

Two of the people baptised that year were Jack and Jean Neville. They became two of Australia's leading literature evangelists.

Let me test your memory. Excluding the former USSR, can you list every city where you've held a major evangelistic series?

I started in New South Wales, Australia, by assisting Eddie Totenhofer in Broken Hill. The next year I went with him to Cowra and Grenfell and Canowindra [pronounced *Ca-noun-dra*] as his assistant. Next year I went to Wagga Wagga and worked on a team with Pastor George Burnside. Then I went to Parkes and ran my first program. The next year was in Forbes, then Canberra, Australia's capital city. After that I went to Taree, Grafton, Maclean, Gosford, Woy Woy, Murwillumbah and Tweed Heads, all in northern New South Wales. Then Mackay, Sarina and Townsville in Queensland. Then Albury, Melbourne and Sydney.

Port Moresby in Papua New Guinea was my first overseas program followed by Manila in the Philippines and Kingston, Jamaica. I ran several programs in Fort Worth, Texas, two in Harare, Zimbabwe. Los Angeles downtown at Shrine Auditorium and in the Los Angeles suburbs of Pasadena, Glendale and Arcadia.

I have also run brief weekend campaigns at Baghdad in Iraq, Amman in Jordan, Cairo in Egypt, in England, Canada and other parts of North America.

You run your meetings in darkness for the first seven nights. Then you turn on the hall lights and give Bibles to everyone in the audience. Why?

I want people to get a Bible in their hands and to get to know the Bible. I want them to experience the power that comes from reading the Scriptures. You can't do that with the hall lights turned out. That's the reason why our program is more successful than others. Everything they do in their meetings is done in the dark.

It's stupidity. That's what [Australian evangelist] George Burnside taught me—and he was right.

In the Adventist Church today there is a huge tendency for young preachers to rely on PowerPoint and all that sort of stuff. They need to develop the ability to preach the Bible and hold the audience with the Bible, like Billy Graham did.

We can't compete with Hollywood, and we shouldn't try. If we compete with Hollywood, they are going to beat us with their big budgets and special effects. But Hollywood can't compete with us because we have the Bible, the Word of God.

When in Russia, you didn't just run evangelistic programs.

That's right. When I ran a campaign in a city, pastors from other cities would come to help. So we rewarded them for assisting us. During the first week of the program, we would hold a workshop for them. These workshops were always about ways they could become more effective in doing their work as pastors. We could run these for only one week, because after the first week those pastors were busy visiting the homes of people who had come to the meetings. But that one week was valuable instruction for the pastors. About 200 pastors have been through the training programs we have held.

How do you reduce the numbers of newly baptised people who leave the church?

I organise the converts into new churches. I often pay the wages of the pastors for the first few months so the conferences will appoint pastors. I pay the rentals on the halls for six or 12 months. I give every church a [music] synthesiser and a PA system. Every new believer gets a Bible. I try to give every new believer the Russian version of the book *Bible Readings for the Home Circle.* And all new converts are visited in their homes, usually several times.

Six months later I go back and take meetings with them. I beg the conferences not to move the ministers around because if they stay, the people are less likely to leave.

What happens to evangelism after one of your campaigns?

I don't know what happens everywhere. However, in some cities the number of baptisms in the years after my meetings has been 50 per cent more than in the years beforehand.

Tell me some stories about people you have baptised.

On my visit to Russia in 2005, one of my team took me out of the city to see a wonderful rehabilitation centre. Here was a man named Valeri, who was baptised four years earlier. He had been an atheist and a member of the Mafia before he joined the church. He then decided he was going to spend the rest of his life helping people who had been like him.

I was amazed when he walked me through his farm buildings. The people there had been the dregs of society. Some were drug addicts, some ex-criminals just released from prison. Others were alcoholics. One of the ex-prisoners I saw there had no legs. He lost them because of the harshness and brutality of prison life. In Russia, people like those at the rehabilitation centre are often considered worthless, despised and rejected. But Valeri doesn't consider them that way. He cares for all of them.

The key to this place was a mushroom farm that raises the money to finance the operation. There are about 30 or 40 people there and they work growing mushrooms. All of them are given three meals a day and a place to sleep. They had all been given Bibles. They had all come out of crime, alcohol and drugs—and given themselves to God. Upstairs in one of their farm buildings they have a church. They meet there three times a day. They were all waiting to hear me preach. I prayed a silent prayer for protection from tuberculosis, the killer of the prisoners. Then I walked up the stairs into this farm room church and told these men and women about the love of God.

You've built churches in the former USSR.

Yes. *The Carter Report* has built six church buildings. That may not sound like a lot, but it is more churches in that part of the world than any other organisation. You can't just run an evangelistic program and walk away from any ongoing responsibility. We make sure we have paid the hall hire for 12 months for each new congregation. And when funds are available, we build church buildings for them.

Could you have baptised many more people?

Sometimes we are too timid in baptising people. At Gorky 10,000 people came forward, but we reduced this number to 2500 because we waited two weeks. I held a baptismal class to make sure they had everything they needed to know before they were baptised. I would say this was too cautious. Possibly if I had baptised the 10,000 when they came forward, we would have more people in the church today.

Aren't people more likely to stay in the church if they study for a longer time before they are baptised?

I have had people who studied a long time before they were baptised, but left the church. And I had some others who studied very little before they were baptised who are still in the church.

There is such a thing as waiting—and waiting too long.

You mentioned earlier that at times you've been depressed.

I think almost all people get depressed at some time, and that includes Christians. The worst depression I ever had was when my 1990 meetings in the Los Angeles Shrine Auditorium were cancelled. We were on track to baptise 3500 people. I quickly started a new church to try to rescue some of these newborn Christians. But they came from all over Los Angeles. My hastily created church could only cater for one locality. So I could rescue only about 300 of them. Because of this experience, I had underlying depression for the next four years. I don't think Beverley is over it yet.

What is the most dangerous thing you have done in Russia?

It is probably carrying cash into the country. Until three years ago, I always carried about $150,000 whenever I went into the country. The banks were often collapsing and it was too much of a risk to try to transfer money through the financial system. But carrying the money was also a huge personal risk. I always declared the cash at the border. I would then be taken into a room by myself and searched. The slabs of American $100 notes would be stacked on a table.

Most of these customs inspectors were corrupt. I would have to slip one $100 note off the pile before they would allow me to leave. That was the price of doing business in Russia. But the biggest danger was the Mafia. I always knew the customs officer might phone the Mafia and tell them about the money. The Mafia might then bundle me into a car as I walked out of the airport terminal. I knew if that happened, there would be only one chance in a million I would survive.

What were the translators at your meetings like?

I remember looking out a window of the Russia Hotel in Gorky about 1996. My translator then was Pastor Igor Pospehin. He started to talk about the view from the window. Then he talked about the hard times in Russia. He talked about when he and his wife, Olga, were baptised. It was held at night to reduce the risk of being caught by the Communists. The church members cut a hole in the ice for them. When they came out of the water, it was so cold their baptismal robes froze solid. Two church members used a knife to cut them free from the robes. Then they covered both of them with blankets and gave them hot drinks to warm their bodies.

Igor talked about the Adventist pastors who'd been killed under Communism and some who'd turned traitor. He talked about the millions of people in the former USSR who had never heard the gospel. He asked me if the churches of America, Australia, New Zealand and Western Europe cared for the 290 million people in the former USSR.

"What do the leaders think? What do the people think? Do they care? Does no-one care?" His question has never left me.

How do you feel when you come back from a campaign in Russia?

I am exhausted for weeks. I'm emotionally drained by what I see. But I am also charged by what we are able to do by God's grace. This is not a game. We are actually touching people's lives. Often our reaction determines how they are going to spend their lives now and in eternity.

Do you consider yourself an American or an Australian?

Sometimes I feel like a Russian! I have dual citizenship, both

Australian and American, but I am primarily a citizen of heaven.

You don't have an Australian accent anymore.

No? Before I left Australia 20 years ago, I went to a speech consultant in Sydney. He taught me to speak international English. That means that wherever I speak, my accent won't be a barrier to people understanding the gospel.

You seem to be a good business manager.

Other folks think I'm a good businessman, which I'm not. We are running a business here. It's God's work, but still it's a business. And God has blessed us with assets. But that's not because I'm a good businessman. It's in spite of me.

People say you're too generous.

No, you can't be too generous. I think there's nothing uglier or more ungodly than stinginess. Staff members have told me "Why do this" when I have given stuff to people and they don't even say thank you. I reply, "Jesus said, 'It's more blessed to give than receive.' And if we can help others to learn the spirit of generosity by our example, we're giving them a great blessing. I would rather be taken for a ride, than to be always suspicious of people."

Tell me about Anna and her child.

Anna was my choir leader in my first series in Nizhni. I returned to that city six months later and there was a knock on my door. Anna was in hospital dying from complications after giving birth to twins. I went to the intensive care unit at the hospital. I prayed with her and I anointed her. But she died that night. And one of her babies died also. What had happened is that the hospital had run out of drugs. The drug needed to keep Anna alive would have cost only $5.

I helped conduct the funeral service. Anna was buried in a cardboard coffin with flowers drawn on the sides. We laid her baby at her breast in the coffin. And the church members stroked her hair before we buried her. Beverley still has a picture of Anna on her bedside table. And for several years, Beverley and I paid for the upkeep of her surviving daughter, who is also named Anna.

What would you like to say to the next generation of pastors?

I think today, from what I can see, most young ministers seem to have an inward-looking church ministry. Instead of what Jesus said, "The field is the world," to them the field is the church. So it goes against the teachings of our Lord who said to "go into all the world." He didn't say, "Go into all the church."

What is the secret of your preaching success?

It's very biblically based. And I don't just quote the Bible. I have the people turn to the texts. I believe the power is in the Bible.

I have often heard you compared to other evangelists. What do you think of competition between evangelists?

We are not competing. We are all on the same team and we should build up the other man. The spirit of competition is carnal and does terrible damage to the church.

Should an evangelist make an appeal in every sermon?

Yes. Appeals should be often and fervent. Appeals should be varied, of course. There are appeals for Christ. There are appeals to accept the Bible. There are appeals to accept the Creator. At the opening meeting dealing with a non-believing audience, the appeal should not be pointed.

What about making appeals in weekly worship services?

I do every week when I preach. H M S Richards's dad called it, "opening the door of the church." That means making an appeal with a view to people becoming members of the church. But you don't have to make the same appeal every week.

There are different types of appeals. There are appeals to make a commitment to read your Bible every day. There are appeals to accept Christ as saviour. There are appeals for us to pray for our lost loved ones, particularly lost children. I ask the parents who are concerned for the salvation of their children to come down the front. Then I specifically pray for the children. There's an appeal for baptism, an appeal for those carrying heavy burdens, an appeal for those struggling with sin, an appeal for those struggling with sickness.

Has the fact that you keep the Sabbath on Saturday reduced the number of people won to Christ at your campaigns?

The Sabbath is a great testing truth. We often hear some Christians say in a derogatory way, "Anyone can keep that old Sabbath." However, it's obvious they have never been in a position where they could lose their jobs if they took a stand for the Sabbath. Therefore the Sabbath becomes a test of our trust in Christ to supply our needs. As it is taught in the Bible, it is a test of our loyalty to God. The Bible says the Sabbath is a sign that we have been saved by faith [see Ezekiel 20:12].

Does the Sabbath have any particular significance for Christians in Russia?

The entire Soviet population was taught for 70 years that man was a machine, a mere animal. That's because of the atheism they embraced. So the Sabbath in Russia has tremendous significance because it tells these people they are children of the Creator God.

The Sabbath is taught all the way through the Bible and tells us where we came from, why we are here, and where we are going.

What is the real John Carter like?

I think what you see is what you get. I've never been called Machiavellian or a schemer. I hope I am transparent—even though I have many faults and I am a sinner. Martin Luther said, "A Christian is always a sinner, always a penitent, and always right with God." I relate to that very well.

Why did you put a cross on your church?

Because the cross of the Lord Jesus is the centre of our faith. And Paul said, "God forbid that I should glory, except in the cross of our Lord Jesus Christ." Our building used to be owned by a different organisation. We wanted to make a statement that we are an evangelical group. Adventist churches around the world have crosses. In Russia, they all have crosses, just like the Dime Tabernacle in Battle Creek that Ellen White helped build.

You have a big emphasis on salvation in your meetings.

Yes. I have a strong, strong, strong conviction that the centre of the Bible is the cross of Jesus Christ. I believe the cross of Jesus Christ explains all mysteries. And more than anything else, it reveals the astounding love of God for the individual.

We are saved by grace alone, through faith alone. We are saved by Christ's works, not our own works.

You have an interesting way of linking salvation with astronomy.

I have read a lot of books about the universe and the vast enormity of space. I tie this in with the cross because the Bible teaches that the man hanging on the cross was the God who made this vast universe. So the cross reveals what the Creator is like: infinitely powerful and infinitely loving.

So in every sermon I preach I try to bring the cross in somewhere. More than anything else, it shows the vastness of the love of God. But not only the love of God. It shows the justice of God because on the cross God in Christ took the sinner's place and was punished for our sins. Thus, the cross shows the holiness of God, the righteousness of God, the justice of God and the extent to which the Creator will go to atone for the sins of His lost children.

From a negative viewpoint, I have through television and in public evangelistic meetings heard a lot of preaching that is purely legalistic. The cross is somehow tacked on at the end of an evangelistic series. That is wrong.

Probably no person has influenced my ministry more than H M S Richards. His great book *Feed My Sheep* emphasises the paramount necessity of preaching Christ crucified. It's the best book in the world on preaching. In the book he talks about people who came to evangelistic meetings and were filled with doctrine. Doctrine is very important, but H M S Richards talks about people becoming dogmatic authorities on the law, the Sabbath, the state of the dead, the prophecies about the antichrist. They could argue those truths until they were blue in the face. However, in their daily lives they were cold, critical and, in the words of one person, they were the "frozen chosen."

Do you credit your success in Russia to your strong emphasis on the gospel?

Absolutely! Legalistic preaching destroys souls. It doesn't save them. In Russia on the second night, when I am talking about archaeology, about the sacrifice places in Petra, I move into the doctrine of atonement. I discovered that as I preached Christ in Russia, I saw vast audiences melting into tears. It really is the power of God unto salvation.

Unfortunately, the word *gospel*, like the word *love*, is one of the most abused words in our language. People talk about preaching the gospel, but often they don't know what the gospel is.

The gospel is the amazing news that the almighty Creator God, who made a trillion billion suns, became a man in Jesus. He felt my pain, experienced my sorrows, and bore the curse of my sins, so that I could be forgiven, acquitted and received back into the Father's fellowship. The gospel tells me that in spite of all my faults, because of Christ I am redeemed, I am secure, I am safe and I am going home to heaven. It is this gospel that breaks hard, stony hearts and wins the lost to God. For the gospel the world is dying.

I am always moved by the story of John Newton, the keeper of slaves who himself became a slave in darkest Africa. He was converted through the prayers of a godly wife and the preaching of the Wesley brothers. We remember him chiefly because of the hymn "Amazing Grace." A short time before his death, he was asked what his doctrines were. He said, "My memory is almost gone and I can remember only two great truths. That I am a great sinner and that Jesus is a great saviour." As far as I am concerned, there are only two great truths. I believe that. Thank God for His amazing grace.

"YOU CAN'T SAVE THE WORLD"

You can't save the world," one of Carter's friends once told him. But you can imagine Carter thinking, *Why not?*

There is a problem when writing the story of someone still alive. Just after you finish writing, that person may do something else that should be included in the story. That is definitely the case with John Carter.

This book may also be a story that ends before its climax. Carter is about to attempt the biggest evangelistic series of his life. Carter's mind has turned to the great nation of India.

Plans are well advanced for the largest evangelistic series attempted by Seventh-day Adventists. It will be on the east coast of India and the scale of the project is awesome.

Organisers are booking a fleet of hundreds of trucks to bring people to the meetings. Each truck can hold 150 people standing shoulder to shoulder. They are planning for an audience of up to a quarter of a million people and hope to establish 50 new churches. Carter would like to baptise as many people in this one campaign as he has in his *entire* career in Russia.

In India today, huge economic change is taking place. The nation is developing rapidly and is now the 10th largest economy on earth. The economic changes the Indian people see all around them subconsciously make them more willing to change their religion.

In the past 10 years, 800,000 people in India have become Seventh-day Adventists. Most of these people, however, were nominal Christians before becoming Adventist Christians. Carter's proposed evangelistic program is different. He is aiming to reach Hindus, the religion followed by 80 per cent of the population.

Carter's first full-scale crusade in Russia cost $US50,000. Today, 15 years later, that crusade would cost a million dollars. It will be the same in India. In a decade's time, we will look back at John Carter's million-dollar crusade in India and say, "I wish we could do it for such a low price today."

The church in India has learned important lessons from mistakes in Russia. The 1992 evangelistic campaign the Adventist Church ran in Moscow was the most successful run in that city by any denomination. However, the Adventists didn't build or buy church buildings for the new converts. By contrast, the Baptists built 50 churches. And they did it when real estate was cheap. Fifteen years ago you could build 20 churches in Moscow for the cost of building one church today. Sadly today, there is only one Adventist Church building in Moscow.

The Carter program in India will not fall into that same trap. The evangelistic series is being held in conjunction with Maranatha International. Carter will do the preaching and Maranatha will build new churches to house the converts. At the moment, it costs only $US11,000 to build a new church that will house 400 people. Because of India's economic boom, the cost of building that same church in a few years time could be $US100,000.

The Carter–Maranatha outreach in India plans to build up to 50 new church buildings. So each of the 50 new congregations, which they hope to form from the Carter series, will have its own house of worship.

Carter's opening program has set evangelistic attendance records on four of the six inhabited continents. He's had the largest opening attendances at Adventist campaigns in Europe (50,000 at Kiev), in North America (24,000 at Los Angeles), in Africa (18,000 at Harare) and in Australia (18,000 at Sydney). He also set the largest ever Adventist evangelistic attendance in a nation that is not part of a continent (30,000 at Manila).

By the time you read this, Carter may have added a fifth continent to the list—the largest ever attendance at an Adventist series in Asia. In fact, if they achieve only a quarter of their opening audience aim of 250,000 people in India, it will be the Adventist Church's largest ever attendance anywhere in the world.

CARTER'S GREAT FRUSTRATION

Russia has 250 cities, and Ukraine 100 more. John Carter has held evangelistic campaigns in 10 of these cities, resulting in about 15,000 baptisms and 60 new churches started (see Appendix). And we have shared many of these stories.

This impact is remarkable; however, for Carter himself, it is only a list of 10 cities out of 350. He is concerned for the 340 cities of Russia and Ukraine where he has never held a public series. And after developing a taste for campaigning in India, now he is also concerned for the half-million cities and villages of India.

"But I'm wearing out," says Carter, who in 2004 retired as a full-time church pastor. "The body doesn't work as well as it used to."

And he has a deeper concern than which city he should or shouldn't preach in. He's worried about what will happen when he passes on. Who will follow his example of lighting gospel fires in city after city?

Statistics for the years 2000-04 show that the Carter team was responsible for 60 per cent of the Adventist Church's evangelistic baptisms in the former USSR. What will happen to church growth there when Carter is unable to run evangelistic programs?

The Carter Report organisation sponsors two Russian evangelists. Carter's fundraising pays their wages and meets the expenses for their evangelistic campaigns. They use the advertising and preaching techniques Carter created and developed. The evangelistic programs run by those two pastors have resulted in more than 10,000 baptisms.

John Carter has proved that the archaeology-based evangelistic technique is successful in Russia, Ukraine and the United States. But he is frustrated because almost no-one wants to duplicate his successful methods. He is not worried about copyright on his advertising. He is happy for other evangelists to use it. He doesn't feel it is wrong for others to reproduce his successful methods. But it isn't happening.

Carter wants to spend his final years passing on the flame. He wants two or three evangelists to go into Russia; two or three in Australia; five or six in the United States; a dozen in Europe. Better still, he wants 100 in each of those areas. He wants to inspire and see evangelists who will go into all nations, using proven techniques to preach the gospel.

The life of John Carter demonstrates the truth of a statement made by Ellen White: "There is no limit to the usefulness of the one who, putting self aside, makes room for the working of the Holy Spirit upon his heart, and lives a life wholly consecrated to God."*

And this must be a challenge to each of us.

Southern Watchman, August 1, 1905.

A NOTE FROM THE AUTHOR

Dear reader,

Let me make this a personal matter.

No matter what you think, you have not been reading just a book. You have been reading a manual. Woven into this adventure are details of how you may be able to do what John Carter has done.

These pages are not just the tale of something in the past. They could be a story of the future—your future. This is not just the story of an Australian church pastor. It could be a story about you, no matter what your nationality. Or it might be the story about young people you know. Pass the book on to them. Let your young friends be inspired by it.

And read the book again yourself. Be thrilled by:

- how God thwarted city officials who tried to close down Carter's meetings;
- how a bodyguard was standing in just the right place to block a Mafia attack on the preacher; and
- how John Carter escaped being shot when he was marched into the bush at gunpoint.

But look even deeper when you read the book again. Search its pages to learn:

- how to attract non-religious people to religious meetings;
- how to imitate successful ideas to spread the gospel;

- how to tell God's message in an exciting way;
- how to reduce the number of newly-baptised people who leave the church; and
- how to lead people to make a decision.

As you read the book again, you will discover dozens of secrets for success in evangelism that are deliberately hidden in these pages.

Apply those ideas. Copy them. Imitate them. Adapt them. Use them.

And you will be blessed.

—*Phil Ward*

APPENDIX

The list of cities where John Carter has held his major programs in Russia and Ukraine is an impressive record. It shows he has baptised an average of more than 1000 people each year.

Year	City	Baptisms
1991	Moscow	*
1992	Gorky (Nizhni Novgorod)	2530
1992	Dzerzinsk	130
1993	Nizhni	1500
1994	Nizhni	1300
1995	Kiev	3488
1996	Nizhni	800
1997	St Petersburg	1000
1999	Irkutsk	762
2001	Dnepropetrovsk	1281
2002	Kharkov	1121
2003	Odessa	650
2004	Zaporozhye	350

Consider a few of the raw statistics from these meetings:

Combined total attendance: 3.5 million people

Free Bibles given away: 250,000

Christian books given away: 150,000

Gospel audiotapes distributed: 250,000

Number of new churches started: 60

Number of converts ordained as pastors: 100

Decisions made for Christ: 100,000

Number of baptisms: 15,000**

*John was instructed not to baptise anyone during his Moscow program. However, 100 people who attended his meetings there were baptised three months later.

**This figure is only the number of baptisms that took place during the actual Carter programs. An estimated 5000 people who attended Carter meetings were baptised in the follow-up Revelation Seminars held after each program. In addition 85,000 people made decisions for Christ but were not baptised. There are no records of how many of these new Christians joined other denominations.

CONTACTING CARTER

In the United States, donations to *The Carter Report, Inc* are tax deductible. If you wish to support John Carter, you can contact his organisation in North America at:

> The Carter Report, Inc
> PO Box 1900
> Thousand Oaks, California, 91358

> The Carter Report, Inc
> 100 W Duarte Road
> Arcadia, California, 91007
> Phone (626) 254 0898

Or in Australia:

> c/- Harold Harker
> PO Box 861
> Terrigal NSW 2260
> Phone (02) 4385 8282

Or on the internet:

> www.cartereport.org